I0605800

SEOUL FOOD

Food is love; it truly is.

This book is for my family.
Thank you for feeding me your food,
and letting me feed you with mine.

Text © 2025 Haebin Sudo
All photography © Simon Smith, except pages 7 and 8 © Shutterstock.com
Jacket illustrations © Asako Masunouchi

The right of Haebin Sudo to be identified as the Author of the Work has been asserted by her in accordance with the Copyright, Designs and Patents Act 1988.

First published in 2025 by OH
An Imprint of HEADLINE PUBLISHING GROUP LIMITED
1

Apart from any use permitted under UK copyright law, this publication may only be reproduced, stored, or transmitted, in any form, or by any means, with prior permission in writing of the publishers or, in the case of reprographic production, in accordance with the terms of licences issued by the Copyright Licensing Agency.

Cataloguing in Publication Data is available from the British Library

ISBN 9781035429677

Printed and bound in China by Toppan Leefung Printing Ltd.

Headline's policy is to use papers that are natural, renewable and recyclable products and made from wood grown in well-managed forests and other controlled sources. The logging and manufacturing processes are expected to conform to the environmental regulations of the country of origin.

HEADLINE PUBLISHING GROUP LIMITED
An Hachette UK Company, Carmelite House, 50 Victoria Embankment, London, EC4Y 0DZ

The authorised representative in the EEA is Hachette Ireland,
8 Castlecourt Centre, Dublin 15, D15 XTP3, Ireland (email: info@hbgi.ie)
www.headline.co.uk / www.hachette.co.uk

SEOUL FOOD

HAEBIN SUDO

FROM KIMBAP TO KIMCHI, DELICIOUS RECIPES FROM THE HEART OF KOREA

OH

CONTENTS
목차

INTRODUCTION

Looking back at my childhood, most of my memories around food involve the hustle and bustle of extended family feasts. Older children helping to prepare food and carrying endless plates to the table as the grown-ups kept cooking in the kitchen. The dishes would be placed on a line of low tables that everyone sat around o s sat on one side of the table and the grown-ups the other. I used to have a small spoonful of rice in between all the different dishes on the table, and I would always run out of rice before I had tried everything!

Having to share main dishes meant that from a young age I learned to read the table and hold back from grabbing the best piece of meat before the others had had a chance to eat first. As a mother of three, I now realise that exposure to these kinds of interactions at dinner tables are the foundation to teaching children how to be considerate and to know specific manners. As with everywhere in the world, these big family feasts are becoming more and more rare and, sadly, children miss out on so much as a result.

As well as the huge extended family feasts, I also fondly remember my favourite quick breakfasts, where I used to pour hot barley tea over a bowl of cold, leftover rice and eat it with roasted seaweed and salty preserved clams. This simple, but powerful taste is so deeply ingrained in my food memory bank that I still sometimes get sudden cravings for it. Funny how it's usually the simplest foods that people long for from their childhood.

In this book, I have arranged all the dishes deliberately to showcase the huge family feasts I used to love, as well as some more casual Korean dishes. The first three chapters each offer a selection of ten dishes that will provide all you need for a sumptuous Korean feast for your family and friends. While these have been carefully curated, there is always room for some mixing and matching, such as swapping vegetable namul dishes or meat dishes between chapters. In the second half of the book, I introduce you to my favourite Korean street-food dishes and easy one-plate meals, before finishing with a chapter on East meets West, Korean fusion food. Come along with me for a truly authentic Korean food adventure!

THE KOREAN DINNER TABLE

Before you start trying out the recipes, a brief background information on how Korean people normally eat their meals will help you make the most of this book. Unlike a typical Western meal, where you usually have various food items together on a single plate, an everyday Korean meal consists of rice and soup per person, with a selection of side dishes called 'banchan' placed in the middle to be shared.

Korea has a long history of being Buddhist, and despite being well known for meaty dishes, it used to be largely vegetarian. All the seasonal vegetable banchan, prepared in a variety of ways and flavoured in simple Korean seasonings, are called 'namul'. There are hundreds of namul dishes consumed daily and they are a huge part of Korean cuisine.

At every meal a typical Korean person will have one or two types of kimchi and two or three banchan, including namul, alongside rice and soup. Banchan are usually prepared in big batches and kept in the fridge for up to a week or two. This enables us to quickly fix a meal, given that there is usually warm rice in the rice cooker. With this base of rice, soup and sides, we create more special meals by adding meaty main dishes and increasing the number of banchan served.

While the first three 'feasts' in this book show you everything you need to host an epic dinner party, just a few dishes from the feast will set up a delicious family dinner. Korean food is, above anything, about the enjoyment of sharing with your loved ones and it is usually very casual. With this in mind, please have fun with this book and go mix and match from different chapters.

The following images are typical Korean meals, from simplest to most elaborate. First, a simple home meal.

Big meal: this is a good example of a large, family weekend meal.

If enjoying a big Korean feast in a restaurant, this is what it might look like.

AN INTRODUCTION TO KOREAN INGREDIENTS

Authentic Korean cooking does require a few specialist ingredients, but they're absolutely worth buying to make your dishes as delicious as possible. Some of these – such as gochujang – have made their way into the mainstream in recent years and can be bought from most supermarkets. Anything not available there will be available in Asian grocery stores or online.

Here are my top Korean cooking ingredients that I use all the time. The first five are the ones I use most frequently and those I recommend investing in as they are very specific to Korean food and I wouldn't recommend using replacements from other cuisines.

SOY SAUCE

When you go to Korean supermarkets, you often see three types of soy sauce: jin-kanjang, yangjo-kanjang and guk-kanjang.

- Jin-kanjang usually says 'Jin Gold F3' on the bottle somewhere. This is the most versatile and most commonly used soy sauce in Korean cooking. Korean soy sauce tastes different from the Japanese and Chinese, so I recommend investing in a bottle. I tend to buy the smallest bottle there is so it stays fairly fresh until I finish it up. After several months, the soy sauce will change its colour and taste. If you do buy a big bottle, you can keep it in a fridge to keep the freshness longer.
- Yangjo-kanjang is a more delicate, slightly sweet tasting soy sauce, but it can change its taste when cooked above a certain temperature, so it is used more for dipping sauce, salad dressings and to season things that don't require extensive cooking.
- Guk-kanjang is the soy sauce for soups. It's lighter in colour but much saltier than the other two. It has less sweetness and more umami and is usually used for making the brothy soups that Koreans eat multiple times a week, so is a must for a Korean pantry.

Korean kitchens will usually have all three or at least two types of the soy sauce. I personally have Jin-kanjang and Guk-kanjang in my pantry.

I recommend using Jin-kinjang for all recipes in this book, unless otherwise specified. As mentioned, it's worth buying a bottle of Jin-kinjang, but at a push you can substitue it with Chinese light soy sauce or – even better – Japanese soy sauce.

GOCHUJANG (KOREAN CHILLI PASTE)

This is a must for Korean cooking and something that we use quite a lot! It's a thick paste that has distinctive sweet and smoky flavours as well as the punch of chillies. There are many brands of gochujang but most of them are similar so you won't go far wrong with whichever one you choose – they can all be used to make all kinds of dishes.

GOCHUGARU (KOREAN CHILLI POWDER)

Gochugaru is a Korean chilli powder that come in two types – rough and fine. The rougher type is used most often, for example when making kimchi. Korean chilli flakes are much milder than those from other cuisines. Fine gochugaru is often used to make food more red and vibrant, but is usually an optional ingredient so don't worry too much if you can't get hold of it.

SESAME OIL

Our talented chef/food stylist for the book could not believe how much sesame oil we went through during our food prep for the photoshoots! Sesame oil is like olive oil to Koreans, and we use it for everything – it is the foundation of traditional Korean taste buds. I sometimes use Japanese sesame oil, which is almost identical, but Korean sesame oil is more aromatic.

CORN SYRUP

Sometimes referred to as cooking syrup, this is used for sweetness and when you want the food to have a nice glaze to it. It is slightly less sweet than caster sugar, but if you don't have any corn syrup you can use sugar, just in a slightly smaller quantity.

KOREAN BLACK PEPPER

All Korean kitchens have one of these bright boxy tins of finely ground pepper. It is slightly less pungent than black pepper and goes well with Korean food. Feel free to skip purchasing this item and use your existing pepper choices.

DASIDA

This is Korea's answer to chicken stock and is often used to create umami in food when making stock from scratch is difficult. I guess the famous cow mascot on its packages tricks everyone, including myself, but this is actually a vegan seasoning, even though it has a distinctive umami taste with a hint of beefiness. Just like chicken stock, it can be used in any kinds of sauces and soups for adding depth. There are many other different types of umami seasonings in Korea but this one is the brand that has been around the longest and most commonly used. If you can't find Dasida, it can be substituted with Asian chicken stock powder.

YONDU SEASONING SAUCE

This is another great umami essence that is made naturally from fermenting soybeans. Vegan and plant-based, this can be used to add more discrete umami to your salads, stir fries and soups. In Korean cooking this is usually used when making the vegetable namul. If you can't find the Yondu brand, you can subsitute this with other umami sauces such as fish sauce.

PLUM SAUCE

Plum extract syrup is often used to make kimchi and meat marinades. Traditionally, fresh asian plums are used to make this condiment, however the shop bottles often only have added flavourings. For that reason, I often skip this and just use sugar instead. Nonetheless, it does give a nice fruitiness to the food and is good for marinating pork and other meats.

ASIAN CHICKEN STOCK POWDER

I usually use Chinese chicken stock powder for cooking Asian food because Western chicken stocks have lots of herbs that clash with the Asian ingredients. This chicken stock can be replaced with Dasida if you don't want any kind of meaty umami flavour to your food. It's worth having in your kitchen as it's used so widely in Asian cooking.

FISH SAUCE

Fish sauce is a huge part of Korean cooking and there are many different regional types available in Korea. It is, however, one of those things that is hard to get your hands on outside Korea. Luckily, our Southeast Asian friends use fish sauce a lot too, and there are a couple of decent fish sauce brands available in most supermarkets that I'm happy to use for making kimchi at home and in other cooking. Fish sauce gives amazing umami depth to food and is one of my favourite seasonings. It's especially good for brothy soups and stews, as well as all the lightly pickled kimchi salads.

OTHER INGREDIENTS

MIRIM
Mirim is a Korean cooking wine, akin to Japanese mirin and Chinese cooking wine, both of which are also made from a rice wine base. These can be used interchangeably.

VINEGAR
Where vinegar is specified in a recipe, you can use any Korean brand of apple or rice vinegar if you can get it. Otherwise, any white wine vinegar or apple vinegar will suffice.

SESAME SEEDS
Sesame seeds are used in almost all Korean cooking, either in the dishes themselves or as a pretty ubiquitous garnish! Most shop-bought seeds come already roasted, but you can roast them in a dry pan one more time to make them even more nutty and aromatic. This also makes them easier to crush in a pestle and mortar when a recipe calls for ground sesame seeds.

SALTED SHRIMP
Heavily salted and fermented shrimps are widely used in Korean cuisine. Sold in jars, they are one of the key ingredients in making kimchi.

MSG
Ajinomoto is a famous Japanese MSG brand that is widely used in all Asian cooking and available in Asian supermarkets.

SALT
This is either listed in the recipes as 'salt' or 'sea salt'. Salt can be any table salt, whereas sea salt refers to salt flakes. Maldon salt is my favourite brand of sea salt and the one I always use.

OILS
As well as sesame oil, I often use neutral oils, such as vegetable, for frying. See individual recipes for details.

PHOTOGRAPH KEY

1. Jin-ganjang
2. Gochujang
3. Gochugaru
4. Korean sesame oil
5. Corn syrup/cooking syrup
6. Korean fine black pepper
7. Dasida
8. Yondu seasoning season
9. Plum syrup sauce

7
DASIDA®
3
wang
태양초
고추
가루
HACCP
5
청정원
끈기를 잡아주는
물엿
CORN SYRUP
700 g
9
백설
100%
국내산 매실
1
샘표
진간장
Sempio
Soy Sauce
4
세계일류상품
오뚜기
100% 통참깨
고소한
참기름
500 ml(4,100 kcal)
양조절이 가능한 안심캡 사용!
8
샘표
요리에센스
연두
순
순식물성 콩발효 에센스
2
O'Food
GOCHUJANG
KOREAN TRADITIONAL
순창
청정원
O'Food
GOCHUJANG
100% 현미 태양초 찰 고추장
NET WT. 17.6 oz (1.1 lb) (500g)
6
해표
純
순
100%
후추
100 g
후추 100 %
Pure Ground Black Pepper Powder

1. BULGOGI
2. SPINACH NAMUL V
3. BEAN SPROUT NAMUL V
4. CARROT NAMUL V
5. MUSHROOM NAMUL V
6. MAK-KIMCHI CABBAGE KIMCH
7. BULGOGI BIBIMBAP
8. COD JEON KOREAN FRITTERS
9. DUBU JORIM TOFU STEAK V
10. SILKEN TOFU JJIGAE

1

FIRST TRADITIONAL KOREAN FEAST

To kick off this book of feasts, I have put together ten iconic dishes for our first traditional Korean spread. In this chapter, we get to create a traditional Korean dinner, featuring famous Korean dishes such as bulgogi and bibimbap. This kind of spread would normally be considered a special table for a dinner party or a family occasion because of the presence of bulgogi (page 16) and bibimbap. Bulgogi is considered special because, in the olden days, beef was not easily accessible to normal people and only eaten a few times a year.

'Namul' is a name Koreans use for any seasonal vegetable side dishes that accompany rice. There are hundreds of these vegetable dishes in Korea and they are a huge part of Korean cuisine. Namul can be enjoyed separately as a standalone dish, and you can use them to create a variety of different meals by choosing three to five dishes from this chapter to serve with rice.

If you have already put in the effort to make three or four namul anyway, I highly recommend doing the small extra step of simply serving a bowl of rice to each guest and letting everyone have fun in creating their own perfect bibimbap!

Cooking time: 20 minutes plus marinating

Spiciness: mild

BULGOGI

Bulgogi is one of the best-known Korean dishes, and one that everyone loves. It is very easy to make with a simple marinade over thinly sliced beef. This is usually sirloin, leg meat, rump or any leaner cut, but the bulgogi marinade gives even the cheaper cuts a tasty transformation! In Korea, you can go to any supermarket or butcher and find bulgogi meat beautifully prepared, sliced paper-thin, ready to be marinated. Elsewhere, it can be somewhat difficult to get your hands on this, so a lot of Korean people living abroad buy chunky pieces of sirloin or rump steak and slice at home. The trick is to partially freeze the meat for an hour or so, making it easier to cut very thinly and evenly without a meat slicer.

SERVES A FAMILY OF 4

- About 700 g (1 lb 8 oz) beef, thinly sliced
- 4 spring onions (scallions), stalks only, sliced diagonally in fine strips
- ½ carrot, julienned
- 1 onion, finely sliced
- About 4 shiitake mushrooms (optional), finely sliced
- Sesame seeds to garnish

Marinade

- 8 tbsp soy sauce
- 10 garlic cloves, crushed or minced
- 2 tbsp rice wine (optional)
- ½ tsp Korean black pepper
- 1 tsp Dasida stock powder
- ½ pear (about 100 g/3½ oz), grated (use a fresh Korean or Asian pear if you can)
- ½ white onion, grated
- 2½–3 tbsp caster (superfine) sugar; use 2½ tbsp if using a Korean pear and 3 tbsp if not
- 3 tbsp sesame oil

METHOD

1. Mix all of the ingredients for the marinade together in a bowl or jug.
2. Place the thinly sliced beef and crushed garlic into the marinade and mix well. Leave it to marinate for at least 15 minutes, or overnight.
3. Prepare the vegetables.
4. Set a frying pan over a medium heat. When the pan is hot, begin to sauté the marinated meat.
5. When the meat is nearly cooked, after about 7–8 minutes, add the julienned vegetables. Stir-fry everything together for another 1–2 minutes.
6. You can serve this on rice as a one-plate meal with a bit of gochujang, kimchi and a sprinkle of sesame seeds, or have it as a shared main dish with other banchan.

Suitable for: vegetarian and vegan

Cooking time: 10 minutes

Spiciness: mild

SPINACH NAMUL

This tasty spinach namul is an ideal component of bibimbap (page 30). I like to use crushed sesame seeds (which I do myself in a pestle and mortar) as this releases more of their aroma and the coarse texture soaks up excess moisture from the spinach, preventing the dish from being too watery.

SERVES 2–3 FOR SHARING

1 x 250 g (9 oz) bag of spinach

Seasoning

½ tbsp soy sauce

⅓ tsp sea salt

1 tsp Yondu savoury seasoning sauce

1 tbsp sesame oil

1 clove garlic, grated (optional)

A sprinkle of black pepper

1 tbsp sesame seeds, crushed or whole, to serve

METHOD

1. Boil 2 litres (4 pts) of water in a saucepan.
2. When the water boils, turn off the heat and empty the spinach into it. Submerge all the leaves in the hot water for only about 10 seconds. The baby spinach leaves are so tender that it is easy to overcook them. If you are using tougher spinach with stems, leave in for 25 seconds. Remove from the pot and refresh under cold water to stop the cooking process.
3. Drain the spinach, wrap in kitchen paper and gently squeeze out as much water as you can.
4. Separate out the leaves and place in a bowl. If you used stemmed spinach, cut it into 6-cm (2½-in) lengths.
5. Add the rest of the ingredients, except the sesame seeds, and mix together.
6. Sprinkle whole sesame seeds or crushed sesame seeds before serving. Enjoy as a side dish or on its own.

Suitable for: vegetarian and vegan

Cooking time: 10 minutes

Spiciness: mild

BEAN SPROUT NAMUL

There are certain vegetables that are typically considered to be more Asian than Western but which are surprisingly common here in the UK. Bean sprouts fall into this category, and it has really surprised me to find them in almost all supermarkets, and very cheaply, too!

The only downside of bean sprouts is that they don't stay fresh very long, even in a fridge.

Other than that, they are versatile, super quick to cook, and tasty. And they are one of the staple vegetables used in Korea for making namul banchan.

I love how Chinese and Japanese dishes use bean sprouts, but this Korean-style recipe is special because bean sprouts are the main event, and it is one of the tastiest ways to eat them.

SERVES 2–3 FOR SHARING

1 x 250 g (9 oz) bag of bean sprouts, lightly washed

Seasoning

1–2 spring onion (scallion) stalks, finely sliced (about 1 tbsp)

1–2 cloves garlic, minced (optional)

⅓ tsp sea salt

2 tbsp sesame oil

1 tbsp soy sauce

⅓ tsp black pepper

1 tsp Yondu seasoning sauce

1 tbsp sesame seeds, crushed

TIP

This is a namul banchan so you can eat it together next to other banchan and rice. Or, you can use this to whip up a bibimbap.

METHOD

1. Boil 2 cups of water in a steamer pot, and steam the bean sprouts for 5 minutes. If you don't have a steamer, just cook them in boiling water for 4 minutes.
2. Remove from the heat and refresh under cold water to prevent overcooking.
3. Drain off as much water as possible without squeezing the sprouts.
4. Place them in a mixing bowl and add all of the seasoning ingredients. Gently mix everything and taste, adding a little more salt if you think it needs it.

This namul is lovely to eat slightly warm, just after cooking, and any leftovers will keep in the fridge for 2–3 days. It's also good cold, eaten as a salad.

Suitable for: vegetarian and vegan

Cooking time: 20 minutes

Spiciness: mild

CARROT NAMUL

Carrots are one of the healthiest vegetables and they are consumed religiously by Korean women to maintain a healthy lifestyle. You can have this carrot namul as a salad, a sandwich filling, or a side dish with rice. And, of course, carrots are one of the main components for bibimbap and japchae too. It is worth multiplying the recipe to make a big batch and use it in multiple ways.

When we cook carrots for bibimbap topping or japchae filling, they are normally simply sautéed in a bit of neutral oil and salt and pepper. But the addition of ginger and lemon juice in this namul recipe gives it a fresh depth and makes it a great sandwich filling or salad, too.

SERVES 2–3 FOR SHARING

1 large or 2 small carrots (about 250 g/9 oz)
2 spring onions (scallions), sliced thinly diagonally
1 tsp ginger, grated
⅓ tsp salt
1½ tbsp olive oil
1½ tbsp lemon juice
1 tbsp sesame oil

METHOD

1. Julienne the carrot and spring onion and place in a mixing bowl.
2. Add the grated ginger, sprinkle the salt over the mixture and gently stir together. Leave for 5 minutes before adding the olive oil and lemon juice and mixing well.
3. Heat the sesame oil in a frying pan, add the carrot mixture and stir-fry for a few minutes until the carrot is soft but still has a little crunch.
4. Taste and add a little more salt if you think it needs it, before serving.

Suitable for: vegetarian and vegan

Cooking time: 20 minutes

Spiciness: mild

MUSHROOM NAMUL

Another classic namul dish that Koreans love is mushroom namul. This can be served as a banchan or added to bibimbap or japchae. In Korea, mushroom namul is usually made with common Asian mushrooms, such as shiitake, oyster, enoki or trumpet mushrooms. Common Western mushrooms, such as chestnut, button or Portobello varieties release a lot of water when cooking and are not usually used to make namul, but that does not mean you cannot use them. Just take a few more minutes when sautéing to let any extra moisture evaporate.

SERVES 2–3 FOR SHARING

10 shiitake mushrooms
4 tbsp sesame oil
½–1 tbsp soy sauce
½ tbsp garlic, crushed
⅓ tsp salt to season
1 spring onion (scallion), stalk only, sliced thinly on the diagonal
½ tbsp sesame seeds

METHOD

1. Wash the mushrooms lightly if dirty, and wipe dry.
2. Slice them finely.
3. Heat a large frying pan on a medium heat, adding 3 tbsp of the sesame oil to it when hot.
4. Add the sliced mushrooms and sauté for 3–5 minutes. The mushrooms will soak up the sesame oil instantly and the pan will look dry. Don't worry, just keep tossing the mushrooms to avoid burning. They will release moisture and steam themselves in the pan.
5. Lower the heat and create a small space in the middle of the pan. Add the soy sauce, remaining tbsp sesame oil and crushed garlic into the space. Let it bubble up gently and toss the mushrooms to mix with the sauce.
6. Sprinkle over the salt and keep stirring until the mushrooms are softened.
7. Add the sliced spring onion and sesame seeds and taste.
8. If needed, add extra soy sauce or salt and serve immediately.

TIP

Don't be afraid to add a little more sesame oil or other oil if you feel like the namul is catching and needs more fat in the pan. It all depends on the mushrooms, and there is no precise amount of oil that's right for this dish.

Cooking time: 2 hours

Spiciness: medium to high

MAK-KIMCHI

SIMPLE CABBAGE KIMCHI

Kimchi can be made from lots of different vegetables – cucumber, radish and spring onion, among others – but cabbage kimchi is the most commonly eaten variety both in Korea and around the world.

In fact, in Korea there is a specific kimchi-making season from November to December, when we make and store a whole year's supply of cabbage kimchi. It starts when the temperature drops to 6–7°C (43–45°F) and continues for two weeks. When the kimchi season hits, families gather and make kimchi together. It is common to see trucks delivering 100–200 cabbages and the entire extended family helping to make kimchi. The whole process takes two days, during which time relatives share various meals together, exchange news and take part in kimchi making.

This somewhat crazy tradition is called 'kimjang', and the kimchi made in this way is called 'kimjang-kimchi'. This is not the only type of cabbage kimchi we eat, but it is our staple supply.
At the end of this process, each family will go home with multiple containers of kimjang-kimchi, which will be put in their kimchi fridge (set to 0–1°C/32–34°F, the ideal temperature for kimchi fermentation), then it's fingers crossed for a tasty kimchi year!

Koreans enjoy kimjang-kimchi throughout the year in different ways. Some dishes are enjoyed with fresher 'young' kimchi and some are made only with more mature kimchi, such as soups and stews. No kimchi goes to waste! It is difficult to make proper kimjang-kimchi outside Korea for various reasons, such as the type and quality of ingredients used and the lack of kimchi fridges.

On top of the robust kimjang-kimchi we also make quicker, simpler types of kimchi in smaller quantities ('mak-kimchi') which takes a fraction of the time to make (about 1.5 hours to be exact!).

Traditional kimjang-kimchi is made with whole cabbages that are halved and lightly pickled for 6–8 hours before seasoning with kimchi paste. Mak-kimchi requires cutting the leaves into bite-size pieces and only needs about one hour of pickling. Most of the kimchi you find on supermarket shelves outside Korea are types of mak-kimchi. Note, this is a standard recipe, but adjust the sweetness, saltiness and fishiness to your taste.

TIP

Kimchi scientists believe that the probiotic count reaches its peak around 7–10 days after making. However, kimchi is already full of good minerals and fibre from day 1, and you should enjoy it wherever you like. Lots of people in Korea prefer the 'fresher', crunchier young kimchi over the mature, more sour, softer kimchi. Alternatively, leave your mak-kimchi to mature for 3–4 weeks in the fridge and it can be used to cook dishes such as kimchi jjigae and kimchi fried rice, which require the punch from more mature kimchi.

SERVES A FAMILY OF 4

1 head chinese cabbage (about 1 kg/2 lb 2 oz)
150 g (5 oz/⅔ cup) kimchi salt
½ carrot, julienned
20 g (¾ oz) spring onions (scallions) or Chinese chives, roughly cut

Kimchi paste

35 g (around 10 cloves) garlic, minced
15 g (about a 2.5-cm/1-in piece) ginger, minced
80 g (about ½) apple (Fuji or Pink Lady varieties work well), peeled and deseeded
50 g (about ½) onion
3 tbsp fish sauce
25 g (1 oz) salted shrimps
2 tbsp Korean plum syrup, or 1 tbsp sugar
1 tbsp cooked rice or glutinous rice paste (mix 60ml of cold water and 1 tbsp of glutinous rice flour and slowly heat until it becomes a thick paste)
2 tbsp gochugaru

METHOD

1. Slice off about 2 cm (1 in) from the top of the cabbage, the leaves should then come off easily.
2. Slice the leaves in half, top to bottom first, then slice each half at a downward angle in diagonal stripes 2–3 cm (1–2 in) thick. You will end up with slanted diamond strips, which gives a more even ratio of hard and soft parts of the leaves in the finished kimchi. Place the leaves in a large mixing bowl.
3. Dissolve 100 g (3½ oz) of the kimchi salt in 1 litre (2 pints) of cold water and pour over the cut cabbage leaves. Mix well.
4. Sprinkle the remaining salt over the leaves and let it salt for 1 hour, mixing every 20 minutes.
5. By the end of the hour the leaves should have released lots of water and become bendy. When the thickest part of the leave can be bent without breaking, it's ready.
6. While the leaves are being salted, add all the paste ingredients, except the gochugaru, to a food processor or mini chopper and blend. If you don't have one, use a pestle and mortar to grind up the solid ingredients, and mix in the liquids. Decant into a bowl and add the gochugaru, leaving for a while to mix with the wet ingredients. The colour of the paste will get redder after 10–20 minutes as the gochugaru soaks up the liquid. Set aside until the cabbages leaves are ready.
7. When the leaves are salted enough, rinse them thoroughly to get rid of any excess salt.
8. Drain the cabbage and squeeze out the water as much as possible to avoid watery kimchi. Place the leaves back into the large mixing bowl.
9. Add the carrot and spring onions to the cabbage.
10. Add the kimchi paste and mix well.
11. Put the kimchi in a sealed glass container and let it sit at room temperature for a day before you put it in the fridge. Try to keep it in the coldest part of your fridge (ideally around 1°C/34°F) and wait 2–3 days before enjoying.

Cooking time: 30 minutes

Spiciness: mild

BULGOGI BIBIMBAP

Bibimbap ('mixed rice') is a rice bowl with an assortment of vegetables, gochugang and sometimes sliced beef and egg, and it is undoubtedly one of the most famous dishes from Korea. However, the perfect colourful bowl of assorted ingredients you see in books and posters is not as commonly eaten as you might think. That fancy version is almost exclusively eaten only at specific restaurants or on special occasions. The more casual, freestyle bibimbap is commonly made at home – we can easily whip up a bibimbap by throwing some namul in a bowl with rice, frying up an egg, and mixing it all up with a dollop of gochujang and sesame oil. A quick and healthy one-bowl meal! This is a classic traditional bibimbap recipe with bulgogi (page 16). The taste created by combining it with all the delicious vegetable namul is just amazing, and the stunning result is worth all the effort!

SERVES 1

One portion bulgogi

A selection of namul, such as bean sprout, carrot, mushroom, spinach or courgette namul

1 tbsp cabbage kimchi

1 soft-fried egg per bowl, sunny side up

200 g (7oz) steamed sticky rice

Bibimbap sauce (per person)

1 tbsp gochujang

1 tbsp soy sauce

½ tbsp sugar

2 tbsp sesame oil

1 tbsp sesame seeds, roasted

METHOD

1. First, make the sauce by mixing together all of the sauce ingredients. Set aside while you prepare the rest.
2. Cook one egg per bowl, sunny side up. Traditionally, the fried eggs for this recipe are usually soft-cooked on a low heat with the yolk slightly runny.
3. Start assembling your bibimbap!
4. Place about 200g of steamed sticky rice in the middle of a large bowl and place a tablespoonful of each namul from this chapter and the bulgogi on top to surround the rice.
5. Place the fried egg in the middle.
6. Add the bibimbap sauce and mix together! You can start with adding half a spoonful of sauce and see if you need more. The amount really depends on how spicy you like it. Korean people who are not keen on spicy food (they exist!) often use only soy sauce and sesame oil to season their bibimbap.
7. Bibimbap is often served alongside a small bowl of soup or stew. In this book I have paired it with silken tofu jjigae (a thicker soup), but it goes really well with simpler soups, such as egg drop soup or Korean miso soup, too.

TIP

Some Korean people mix their bibimbap using chopsticks rather than a spoon because they really don't like their bibimbap overmixed.

Cooking time:
less than 30 minutes

Spiciness:
mild

COD JEON

KOREAN FRITTERS

Koreans are big seafood lovers and we eat all kinds of seafood in all kinds of ways. These cod fritters are normally served on traditional family holidays, and I used to love helping the grown-ups make them at family gatherings when I was a child. This recipe calls for simple ingredients and is easy to prepare, but makes the most delicious fish dish! It's a great change from your normal Friday night cod and chips!

SERVES 2–3

300 g (10½ oz) fresh cod fillet
Salt and pepper to season
3–4 tbsp plain (all-purpose) flour
2 medium (US large) eggs
Neutral vegetable oil for frying

Dipping sauce (optional)

2 tbsp soy sauce
½ tbsp vinegar
1 tsp gochugaru
1 tsp sesame seeds

METHOD

1. Slice the cod against the grain of the fish into pieces about 1 cm (½ in) thick.
2. Spread the fish on a plate and season with salt and pepper.
3. Leave to season for 5 minutes and dab dry any excess moisture created.
4. Place the flour in one bowl and, in another, beat the eggs with a pinch of salt.
5. Lightly coat each piece of cod with the flour and then dip into the egg mix to coat with the egg.
6. Heat 3–4 tbsp neutral oil in a frying pan on a medium–low heat.
7. Cook the fish on both sides until golden brown.
8. You can eat the fritters as they are or enjoy with a little dipping sauce. Combine the dipping sauce ingredients in a small bowl for a tasty condiment, or feel free to experiment with your other favourite sauce mixes too!

Suitable for: vegetarian and vegan

Cooking time: 30 minutes

Spiciness: medium

DUBU JORIM

TOFU STEAK

Tofu has been a great staple source of protein for centuries in Asia, and there are many great tofu dishes to explore from all the Asian countries. This one has a uniquely Korean taste due to its sauce. The combination of savoury, sweet and spicy makes this an amazing vegan dish to accompany rice. I am a big meat lover but this is a very satisfying alternative to meat, and it's amazing as the main protein for a vegan bibimbap.

SERVES 2

1 pack (around 350 g/12 oz) medium to hard tofu
A few pinches salt
2 tbsp plain (all-purpose) flour
Neutral vegetable oil for frying
Sliced spring onion and sesame seeds to garnish

Sauce

3 tbsp soy sauce
1 tbsp sugar (or alternative sweetener of your choice)
½ tbsp garlic, minced
2 spring onions (scallions), stalks only, finely chopped
1 tbsp gochugaru
1 tsp sesame seeds
1 tbsp sesame oil
1 tbsp water

METHOD

1. Take the tofu from its packaging and let it sit for a while so the excess water seeps out. You can put a plate on top with something heavy on it to get more water out.
2. Cut the tofu into slices and spread out on a plate.
3. Season the tofu with salt and let it sit for 5 minutes before dabbing it dry with a kitchen towel.
4. Put the flour in a shallow bowl and thinly coat each piece of tofu on all sides.
5. Heat a generous amount of neutral oil (about 3–4 tbsp) in a frying pan on medium to high heat. You can add more later if all the oil is soaked up by the tofu.
6. When the pan is hot, arrange the tofu pieces in it and shallow fry on both sides until golden brown. This will take some time because the tofu still has a lot of moisture in it. It may take about 5 minutes or more on each side.
7. While the tofu pieces get crispy in the pan, mix all of the sauce ingredients together in a bowl.
8. Once the tofu is cooked and has a nice crust on the outside, lower the heat and pour in the sauce. Cover and let it simmer in the sauce for a few minutes.
9. As the sauce thickens, flip the tofu slices a few times to let them get coated evenly.
10. To serve, place the tofu slices on a plate and sprinkle some sesame seeds and spring onion over as a garnish.

Cooking time:
30 minutes–1 hour

Spiciness:
medium to high

SILKEN TOFU JJIGAE

Korean people are obsessed with all kinds of soups and stews, and it's common to have them at almost every meal. What we call soups are generally light broths made with all kinds of meats and vegetables. 'Jjigae' is the name we use for soups with a thicker consistency that are more heavily seasoned and have less broth and more solids; jjigae is also usually served in small stone soup pots to keep it piping hot until the end of the meal and is placed in the middle of the table to share. Regular soups are served one bowl per person.

Silken tofu jjigae is one of the most popular jjigae, and there are many versions of it. Here, I have picked a minced pork version, which you can replace with any meat or seafood (prawns, squid, clams). If you are a vegetarian, you can skip the animal protein and have the tofu only, and maybe consider adding some mushrooms to give an umami boost.

SERVES 4

150 g (5 oz) minced pork
Few pinches salt
300 g (10½ oz) silken tofu
2 tbsp sesame oil
2–3 spring onions (scallions), stalks only, cut diagonally into batons
1 tbsp garlic, crushed
1 tbsp gochugaru
1 tbsp soy sauce
½ large white onion (about 150 g/5 oz) cubed into 2 x 2-cm (1 x 1-in) pieces
⅓ courgette (zucchini) (about 80 g/3 oz) cubed into 2 x 2-cm (1 x 1-in) pieces
500 ml (1 pt) water
1 tbsp fish sauce
1 tsp Dasida stock powder
⅓ tsp Korean black pepper

METHOD

1. Season the pork with a few pinches of salt and set aside.
2. You can use any type of silken tofu for this recipe. If you decide to use a Korean one, it is easy to spot it in Asian stores as it is the only type of tofu sold in a tube. It is somewhat tricky to open these without making a mess; the trick is to slice the package in half and push the tofu out into a bowl. Let the tofu release excess water before using it in the soup.
3. To cook the jjigae, take a small heavy-bottomed pan and set on a medium heat.
4. Add the sesame oil, chopped spring onion and garlic.
5. Stir-fry for 2 minutes until the oil bubbles and the aromatics are released.
6. Add the gochugaru and mix well.
7. Add the seasoned minced pork and keep stirring.
8. When the meat is about half cooked,

after about 5 minutes, add the soy sauce and keep stirring.

9. Add the onions and courgette and stir-fry for a further 2–3 minutes.
10. Add the water, cover and simmer for about 5–10 minutes.
11. Season with the fish sauce, Dasida stock powder and Korean black pepper.
12. Roughly slice the silken tofu into 2-cm (1-in) cubes and add to the soup.
13. Let it all come to a boil again and serve.
14. You can serve it in the pot it was cooked in or served in individual bowls.
15. Mix into steamed rice and enjoy!

1. **TTEOKGALBI** KOREAN SHORT BEEF PATTIES
2. **PRAWNS AND ASPARAGUS JEON** KOREAN FRITTERS
3. **KOREAN-STYLE SMASHED CUCUMBER SALAD**
4. **KIMCHI JJIGAE** KIMCHI STEW
5. **SPICY CHICKEN STEW**
6. **RADISH CUBE KIMCHI**
7. **KOREAN STEAMED EGGS**
8. **GREEN BEANS IN SESAME DRESSING** V
9. **VEGETARIAN JAPCHAE** V
10. **COURGETTE JEON** ZUCCHINI FRITTERS V

SECOND TRADITIONAL KOREAN FEAST

This chapter presents another great example of a typical Korean dinner party spread, featuring traditional dishes that you can proudly serve to your guests. You can pick and mix vegetable namul dishes from other chapters to add to it as you wish. Remember, you can create a balanced Korean meal if you stick to the simple formula of rice, a soup and two to three side dishes. You can make a meal more special by adding some meaty main dishes and extra namul to the base set. 'Japchae' is a staple dish for special occasions in Korea due to its beautifully colourful presence. Although it is considered a lengthy dish to make, just follow my fail-proof recipe step by step for the most delicious japchae!

Cooking time:
1 hour

Spiciness:
mild

TTEOKGALBI

KOREAN SHORT BEEF PATTIES

Tteokgalbi are similar to burger patties in that they use minced (ground) beef. This is considered a royal dish because it was originally created for and served to kings. Originally, the best cuts of beef rib were removed from the bone, minced and seasoned, then moulded back round the bone to be cooked. This recipe has been adapted for an easier cooking process! Ask your butcher to mince your favourite cut of beef or simply get some minced beef from the supermarket. These patties are a real treat in my home and disappear from the plate in minutes!

SERVES A FAMILY OF 4

Neutral vegetable oil
150 g (5 oz) white onion, finely diced
3 spring onions (scallions), stalks only, finely chopped
500 g (1 lb 2 oz) minced (ground) beef
1 tbsp rice powder
1 tbsp garlic, minced
4 tbsp soy sauce
1 tbsp sugar
2 tbsp sesame oil
1 tbsp mirim
½ tsp Korean black pepper
1 tbsp pine nuts, ground to serve

Sauce

100 ml (3½ fl oz/scant ½ cup) water
2 tbsp soy sauce
1 tbsp sugar
1 tbsp mirim
½ tsp Dasida stock powder

METHOD

1. Heat up a frying pan with a drizzle of neutral oil on a medium heat.
2. Sauté the onion and spring onion for a few minutes with a pinch of salt.
3. Add to the beef, the rice powder and remaining ingredients in a mixing bowl.
4. Mix everything thoroughly by hand or with a wooden spoon until the meat becomes a smooth paste.
5. Make round patties with the seasoned meat – you should be able to make about 10 egg-sized patties.
6. Separately, add all of the sauce ingredients to a small bowl, mix together and set aside.
7. Add a tablespoon more oil to the frying pan. On a medium heat, cook the patties for about 5 minutes on each side, depending on their size.
8. When cooked, pour over the sauce and cover. Leave to simmer for 2–3 minutes until the sauce thickens slightly.
9. Serve with a sprinkle of ground pine nuts (or sesame seeds if you don't have pine nuts) as garnish.

TIP

These go perfectly with rice, of course, but work great as a burger too. Sandwich between some brioche bread, with cheese and some lettuce… delicious!

Cooking time:
30 minutes

Spiciness:
mild

PRAWN AND ASPARAGUS JEON

KOREAN FRITTERS

'Jeon' is the name given to a Korean dish similar to fritters in the West. A jeon can be vegetarian or made with all kinds of meat or seafood, usually mixed with additional chopped vegetables. These ingredients are then stirred into a batter and cooked into little pancake-shaped fritters. Usually considered a traditional dish for special occasions, this is a casual version that is easy and quick to make. Kids LOVE them!

SERVES 2–3

150 g (5 oz) fresh or frozen prawns
3 spears asparagus (about 80 g/3 oz)
⅓ onion (about 80 g/3 oz)
⅓ carrot (about 80 g/3 oz)
⅓ tsp salt
⅓ tsp Korean black pepper
2 medium (US large) eggs
4 tbsp plain (all-purpose) flour
3–4 tbsp vegetable oil for frying
Thinly sliced fresh red chilli to add to the batter (optional but highly recommended)

Dipping sauce (optional)

2 tbsp soy sauce
½ tbsp vinegar
½ tsp gochugaru
½ tsp sesame seeds

METHOD

1. Cut the prawns into 1-cm (½-in) pieces and finely dice the asparagus, onion and carrot – you can use a chopper if you have one – and place in a large mixing bowl with the eggs, flour and salt. Mix well.
2. Heat a generous amount of vegetable oil in a large pan over medium–low heat.
3. Spoon 1–2 spoonfuls of the mix into the shape of a small pancake, about 8–9-cm diameter (3½-in). Repeat until you have used up all the mix.
4. Cook on both sides until golden brown. Remove to a plate with kitchen paper to absorb excess oil.
5. These are delicious on their own, but if you are a dipping sauce kind of person, why not try mixing up the ingredients listed in a small bowl.

Cooking time: 15 minutes

Spiciness: medium

KOREAN-STYLE SMASHED CUCUMBER SALAD

This is my take on the famous Sichuan dish, smashed cucumber. The dressing is very typical of Korean flavours and goes perfectly with the way you prep the cucumbers. Many supermarkets carry Persian cucumbers these days – I highly recommend using them. If you are using normal big salad cucumbers, scrape out the seedy, watery insides, and just use the firm fleshy part. Also, if you are using the salad cucumber, it's better to roughly slice it into bite-sized pieces rather than smashing it. Either way, in just 5 minutes, you can make the most refreshing, tasty cucumber salad, which you may find impossible to stop munching on.

SERVES 3–4

3 Persian cucumbers (around 300 g/10½ oz)

Dressing

½ tsp salt

2 tbsp fish sauce

1½ tbsp soy sauce

½-1 tbsp sugar

1½ tbsp gochugaru (adjust for preference)

½ tbsp garlic, minced

1 tbsp ground sesame seeds, and extra for garnish

2 tbsp sesame oil

1–2 spring onions (scallions), stalks only, finely chopped

METHOD

1. Wash the cucumbers and pat dry. If using salad cucumbers, cut in half lengthways and de-seed.
2. In a mixing bowl, add all the ingredients for the dressing and mix together.
3. On a large board, smash the cucumbers gently with a rolling pin and hand-pull into bite-sized pieces.
4. Mix the cucumber and dressing together thoroughly.
5. Sprinkle some more sesame seeds as a garnish.

TIP

Hit the cucumbers just hard enough to crack the outer skin but gentle enough to avoid smashing the insides. You want to keep the salad crunchy and juicy, but create just enough rough edges that will hold on to the dressing nicely.

Cooking time: 30 minutes to 1 hour

Spiciness: medium to high

KIMCHI JJIGAE

KIMCHI STEW

Kimchi jjigae is one of the most famous of Korean soups. Koreans grow up eating this soup from a young age, and the first spoonful of spicy, sour, savoury soup mixed with sweet steamed rice is ingrained in our brain and makes us crave it in our adulthoods – I personally find it hard to go more than a couple of months without it! There is nothing more satisfying and comforting than the first big spoonful of scorching hot kimchi jjigae poured onto some soft sticky rice. It truly is the number one soul food for so many Koreans.

If you are a home kimchi maker and have some mature kimchi (older than 2 months), great! Otherwise, any Korean-brand kimchi would be good for this recipe.

SERVES 4

2 tbsp sesame oil

½ tbsp garlic, crushed

200 g (7 oz) pork belly or shoulder, cut into bite-sized pieces

2 tbsp soy sauce

1 tsp gochugaru (optional)

300 g (10½ oz) mature kimchi, sliced into 3–5-cm (1–2-in) pieces

½ onion, cubed

500 ml (1 pt/generous 2 cups) water

1 tbsp fish sauce

½ tsp Dasida stock powder

½ tbsp sugar

200 g (7 oz) medium to soft tofu (optional)

METHOD

1. Take a heavy-bottomed lidded pot.
2. Set it on a medium to high heat, and add the sesame oil, garlic and pork.
3. Stir-fry to let the meat cook and release its fat. Lower the heat if it starts to catch as burning it will make the soup bitter.
4. Add the soy sauce to season the meat. If you like things spicy, add the gochugaru at this stage too. Stir for a few minutes.
5. Next, add the kimchi pieces and onion, and stir-fry for a further 3 minutes or so to incorporate everything.
6. Add the water, cover and simmer for 10–15 minutes minimum. You can leave it to simmer gently on a low heat for up to 30 minutes to really release and deepen all the flavours.
7. Season with the fish sauce, Dasida and sugar.
8. If using, slice the tofu and lay on top of the soup and let it simmer for another 5 minutes.
9. Serve with sticky rice and enjoy!

TIP

This recipe is really just a guideline. Every kimchi has a different level of tanginess and saltiness, so you have to adjust the amount of all the seasonings to your taste. Luckily this is a very forgiving dish. If it ends up too salty, simply add more water; if it does not have enough umami, add more fish sauce or stock powder.

Cooking time:
1 hour

Spiciness:
high

SPICY CHICKEN STEW

If you've only ever fried chicken or cooked it in the oven, please try this recipe. It's best to use chicken with bones and skin on for a richer flavour. This makes such a wonderful wholesome meal out of simple chicken, and the combination of the sweet gochujang sauce and soft potato is something you simply must try. Like all stews, often the leftovers taste better the next day.

SERVES 4–5

1.5 kg (3 lb 5 oz) chicken pieces, thighs or drumsticks, bones left in
2 carrots
4 large potatoes
4–5 spring onions (scallions), stalks only
2 medium white onions
2 fresh red chillies
600 ml (1¼ pts/2½ cups) water
1 tbsp sesame oil
Sesame seeds to garnish

Paste for the stew

3 tbsp gochujang
2–3 tbsp gochugaru
2 tbsp garlic, crushed
2.5-cm (1-in) piece ginger, grated
4 tbsp soy sauce
½ tbsp Dasida stock powder
2 tbsp fish sauce
3 tbsp sugar
½ tsp Korean black pepper

METHOD

1. Add the chicken to a large pan of water and bring to the boil. Once boiling, remove the chicken and rinse clean under cold running water.
2. While the chicken comes to a boil, mix all the stew paste ingredients together in a bowl.
3. Place the chicken in a large saucepan or casserole and coat in the paste. Mix well and set over a medium heat with the lid on to simmer for 5–10 minutes while you prepare the vegetables.
4. Wash and peel the carrot and potatoes and cut them into chunks. Slice the red chillies and cut the spring onions (scallions) into 5-cm (2-in) lengths and the onion into thick slices.
5. Add the carrot and potatoes to the pot. Pour over the water, cover and simmer for 20 minutes on a low-medium heat.
6. Add the onion, chilli and spring onion and simmer for another 10 minutes with the lid removed until the sauce thickens and the vegetables are soft.
7. Serve on a large serving plate with some sesame seeds to garnish, and enjoy with steamed sticky rice.

Cooking time:
1.5 hours

Spiciness:
medium

RADISH CUBE KIMCHI

Radish kimchi is one of the easier and quicker kimchi to make, and you can start eating it straight away without waiting for it to mature. Like most types of kimchi, time does add magic to it, however, and it will taste better after a few days. Radish kimchi only requires about 30 minutes of pickling, and the whole process can be done within one hour.

The single vital component of a good radish kimchi is the quality of the daikon radish (mooli). Always go for one with a dense feel and green tint at the top.

SERVES A FAMILY OF 4

1 daikon radish (mooli), about 800 g to 1 kg (1 lb 12 oz–2 lb 3 oz)
50–60 g (2–2½ oz) coarse sea salt, depending on the size of the radish
2½ tbsp gochugaru

Kimchi paste

7–10 cloves garlic (blended with other ingredients)
2-cm (¾-in) piece ginger
1 tbsp sugar
1 tbsp plum syrup
3 tbsp fish sauce
1½ tbsp salted shrimp
½ white onion
2 tbsp cooked rice or rice powder paste
2 spring onions (scallions) stalks only, roughly sliced diagonally

METHOD

1. Peel the radish and cut into cubes of 2 cm x 2 cm (1 in x 1 in) size.
2. Sprinkle 50 g (2 oz) of coarse kimchi salt over the radish. Leave to pickle for about 30 minutes, turning it a few times.
3. When it's pickled enough (still crunchy but wilted), drain well and add the gochugaru. Mix well to coat. The gochugaru will dye the radish pieces a deep red.
4. To make the paste, add all of the ingredients to a food processor or a blender and blend to an even consistency.
5. Mix this paste into the pickled radish cubes.
6. Eat straight away or leave in a sealed glass jar at room temperature for a night, then keep in the fridge and eat it chilled.

Cooking time:
20 minutes

Spiciness:
mild

KOREAN STEAMED EGGS

A simple dish that every egg-lover will appreciate, this is probably one of the most popular egg dishes in Korea. There is something about these fluffy, soft and savoury eggs that just gives you a warm feeling inside. Sometimes, this dish is called 'Egg bomb' because the way it is cooked makes the eggs so fluffy that they often overflow from the top of the pot. We usually cook this egg dish in Korean stone pots or heavy-bottomed earthenware pots. It is delicious mixed into steamed rice, but you can also enjoy it on its own. Because of the gentle, mild savoury taste, these steamed eggs are often cooked to be served with really spicy food to calm your palate between bites.

SERVES 3–4 (USUALLY 2 EGGS PER PERSON)

6 medium (US large) eggs

Seasoning

½ tsp sea salt

1 tbsp sesame oil

1 clove garlic, minced (optional)

½ tsp Dasida stock powder

½ tbsp fish sauce

1 tbsp finely chopped carrot, plus a little extra to garnish

1 tbsp finely chopped chives/spring onion (scallion), plus a little extra to garnish

Sesame seeds and drizzle of sesame oil to serve

METHOD

1. Beat the eggs in a large bowl.
2. Add all ingredients and mix well. Leave some diced carrot and chive to use as garnish later.
3. Heat half the amount of water as egg mix in a small heavy-bottomed pan.
4. When the water comes to a boil, add in the eggs.
5. On a medium heat, stir gently until the eggs look about 70 per cent cooked.
6. Lower the heat, sprinkle over the saved vegetable garnish and cover.
7. You will see the egg mix bubble up after a few minutes, when the eggs are completely cooked. By this stage, when you lift up the lid, you will see very fluffed up eggs ready to be served. Sprinkle over some sesame seeds and drizzle sesame oil before serving.

Suitable for: vegetarian

Cooking time: 10–15 minutes

Spiciness: mild

GREEN BEANS IN SESAME DRESSING

I am not sure why, but green beans are not all that common in Korea. However, they have become one of the staple vegetables that I always keep in my fridge in the UK. They are so versatile and tasty, and I love them because they go with so many things. This is a simple green bean banchan that can be eaten as a salad or as a side dish. The sesame dressing goes so well with green beans and with so many other vegetables, such as broccoli, cauliflower, carrots, tomatoes, cucumbers and spinach. Make a bottle of this dressing and it will last two to three weeks in the fridge. You can put it on all kinds of vegetables, and even add some noodles to make a noodle salad.

SERVES 3–4

300 g (10½ oz) green beans

Sesame dressing

- 5 tbsp sesame seeds
- ⅓ tsp salt
- 3 tbsp mayonnaise
- 1 tbsp apple cider vinegar
- 1 tbsp lemon juice
- ½ tbsp sugar
- 1 tbsp soy sauce
- 2–3 sprinkles Asian chicken stock powder or Ajinomoto (Japanese umami seasoning)
- Black pepper, a few sprinkles

METHOD

1. Prepare the green beans by steaming or blanching for 5 minutes until tender, and then refresh in cold water.
2. To make the dressing, use a pestle and mortar to grind the sesame seeds into a fine powder, and then add all the other ingredients and mix together to create a creamy sauce. You can adjust the amount of sugar, salt and vinegar to your own balance of sweetness, saltiness and sourness. Don't be scared to experiment because this is a very forgiving dressing to make, and even if you don't quite get the balance, it will still taste amazing, I promise!
3. Simply toss the green beans in the dressing and serve!

Suitable for:
vegetarian and vegan (see options)

Cooking time:
40 minutes to 1 hour

Spiciness:
mild

VEGETARIAN JAPCHAE

I decided to put the vegetarian version of japchae in this chapter to add some variety. There are many rich meaty dishes in this chapter's suggested feast, and sometimes it's nice to have a lighter dish. 'Japchae' literally means 'mixed thin slices', where all the ingredients are julienned and mixed up with glass noodles. It is savoury, gentle and an amazing way to consume lots of different vegetables. Japchae is one of those main dishes that always features on party tables because it is visually stunning with its array of vibrant colours.

If you are a vegan, just omit the egg sheet topping and oyster sauce. Alternatively, if you would like to add some meat, it is typically made in Korea with lean pork loin, cut into thin strips, marinated in soy sauce and garlic and sautéed.

Finally, I suggest you follow this guidance loosely. You can use as few (or as many) vegetables as you want; as long as the noodles are seasoned well, it will taste great either way.

SERVES A FAMILY OF 4

250 g (9 oz) japchae noodles
1 large carrot, julienned
1 red and 1 orange romano pepper, julienned
1 onion, sliced finely
100 g (3½ oz) shiitake mushroom (optional), sliced finely
1 clove garlic, minced (optional)
200 g (7 oz) baby spinach (optional)
2 medium (US large) eggs (optional)
Salt, pepper and soy sauce for seasoning
Vegetable and sesame oil for cooking

Noodle seasoning

⅓ tsp salt
1 tbsp garlic, crushed
5 tbsp soy sauce
½ tbsp oyster sauce, optional
2 tbsp sugar
1 tbsp corn syrup (you can replace this with ½ tsp extra sugar), the syrup adds shine to the noodles
½ tsp Dasida stock powder
4 tbsp sesame oil
½ tsp Korean black pepper

METHOD

1. First, to make the noodle seasoning, combine all the ingredients together in a large mixing bowl.
2. This dish can be cooked using only one wok. First, heat up a tablespoon of oil and sauté the vegetables in order of hardness: carrots then onions and peppers. Add a little more oil

as needed with each addition of vegetables. When all is sautéed and softened, season with a little salt and pepper. Set aside in a big mixing bowl to cool down and let the excess moisture evaporate.

3. If using, add the shiitake mushrooms, sautéing them in the same pan you used for the other vegetables. Heat 2 tbsp of sesame oil in the pan and add the minced garlic before adding the mushroom slices and sautéing for about 5–10 minutes until they become soft. Add a pinch of salt and ½ tbsp of soy sauce to season at the end. Put aside in the same mixing bowl with other vegetables.
4. If you are using baby spinach, blanch for 10 seconds and refresh in cold water. Squeeze out as much water as you can. Season it with 1 tbsp of sesame oil, a pinch of salt black pepper, and ½ tbsp of soy sauce. Add this to the mixing bowl, too, and all the vegetables are ready!
5. Now fill up the wok with water and bring to a boil. Add the japchae noodles and cook for 7 minutes. Drain and wash under cold water to get rid of any excess starch on the noodles.
6. Return the noodles to the wok, add the sauce and warm on a medium heat.
7. Mix well until the noodles absorb all the sauce and become coloured and seasoned. This process may take 3–5 minutes.
8. Time to mix everything! Add the noodles to the mixing bowl and cut a few times if they are too long and difficult to handle. Mix the noodles and vegetables well with a pair of large tongs.
9. Finish off with a drizzle of sesame oil and some sprinkles of sesame seeds before serving.
10. It's best to serve when it's still warm, but japchae is often eaten cold too. It can keep in the fridge for about 2 days and makes a great leftovers lunch! You can add some chilli sauce when you reheat it and turn it into a spicy topping for a bowl of rice.

OPTIONAL EGG SHEET TOPPING

You can omit this part but it does make the dish look extra special.

1. Beat the eggs and season with a pinch of salt.
2. Heat a large frying pan over a medium heat and add a small amount of oil.
3. Pour the egg into the pan and spread thinly into a pancake shape. It will only need a couple of minutes to cook. Turn off the heat after flipping the egg sheet.
4. Take it out from the pan and rest it on a chopping board. Cut in half to make a semi-circle, then place one on top of the other. Cut the semicircles sheets once more lengthwise, creating four strips of egg. Slice them widthwise as thinly as you can to make thin matchstick shapes. Sprinkle over the noodle dish.

Suitable for: vegetarian

Cooking time: 30 minutes

Spiciness: mild

COURGETTE JEON

ZUCCHINI FRITTERS

This is one of the typical traditional festive dishes we cook in Korea on New Year's Day or lunar festivals, when extended families gather. There are a few stages involved and the process can be considered tedious, especially if you have to make 100 of them for a family gathering! But this is a job typically given to younger members of the family, where they may sit around the table with a production line going, each doing a part, chatting and catching up. And although time-consuming, the reward more than makes up for it. Many courgette haters have been said to be converted after trying one of these!

SERVES 2

- 1 medium courgette (zucchini)
- Salt and pepper
- 2 medium (US large) eggs, beaten
- 2 tbsp plain (all-purpose) flour
- 3–4 tbsp vegetable oil

Dipping sauce (optional)

- 2 tbsp soy sauce
- ½ tbsp vinegar
- ½ tsp gochugaru
- ½ tsp sesame seeds

METHOD

1. Slice the courgette into disks around 8 mm (⅓ in) thick.
2. Spread the slices on a plate and lightly season with salt and pepper.
3. Wipe dry any excess water that comes out after seasoning.
4. Place the flour and eggs in separate deep plates and season the eggs with a pinch of salt.
5. Coat each courgette slice in flour first and then dip into the egg mix.
6. Set a large frying pan on a medium heat and add the vegetable oil.
7. Pan fry the dipped courgette slices, cooking both sides until golden brown. Adjust the heat if they start burning.
8. If you want the dipping sauce, which I recommend, simply mix up the ingredients in a small bowl.
9. Line up the courgette slices nicely to serve along with the dipping sauce, if using.

1. **SPICY PORK**
2. **GALBI-JJIM** SHORT RIB STEW
3. **ROLLED OMELETTE** V
4. **CUCUMBER SALAD IN SESAME DRESSING** V
5. **SHREDDED DAIKON KIMCHI SALAD**
6. **BEEF AND SEAWEED BIRTHDAY SOUP**
7. **COURGETTE NAMUL** V
8. **STEAMED AUBERGINE NAMUL** V
9. **JAPCHAE WITH PULLED GOCHUJANG CHICKEN**
10. **SEAFOOD PAJEON** KOREAN SEAFOOD PANCAKE

CELEBRATION FEAST

The star dish in this feast is the seaweed birthday soup – an iconic Korean dish that's as synonymous with birthdays in Korea as birthday cake is in the West. As well as the birthday soup, the rest of this chapter is put together with other celebratory special dishes, like the short rib stew, pajeon and japchae. You can mix and match any of these dishes to welcome your guests or to feed your family on a special day.

Cooking time:
30 minutes

Spiciness:
medium to high

SPICY PORK

Korean people absolutely adore pork, and this is a classic pork dish that we love to have with rice, wrapped in lettuce leaves. The sauce is a classic gochujang base sweet sauce that goes so well with rice and vegetables. You can pre-make a big batch of this sauce and keep it in the fridge for up to two weeks to use with your favourite form of protein. This dish can be one of the main dishes for a large spread party meal or can be a simple one-bowl dinner with some rice.

SERVES 3–4 PEOPLE

- 500 g (1lb 2oz) pork shoulder
- 1 tbsp mirim
- 2 tbsp soy sauce
- 1 tbsp oyster sauce
- Salt and pepper, to taste
- 1 medium onion
- 1 carrot
- ½ large courgette (zucchini)
- 3 spring onions (scallions), stalks only, cut diagonally in batons
- 1 red chilli (optional), sliced finely
- Salt and pepper to season
- Neutral vegetable oil for frying
- Sesame seeds

Gochujang sauce

- 1 tbsp garlic, crushed
- 2 tbsp soy sauce
- 1 tbsp sugar
- 2 tbsp Korean plum syrup (can be replaced with 1 tbsp of sugar)
- 2 tbsp gochujang
- 1½ tbsp fine gochugaru
- ⅓ tsp Korean black pepper

METHOD

1. Cut the pork shoulder into thin strips. It is much easier to cut thinly if you freeze the meat slightly for about 1 hour and cut when semi-frozen.
2. Marinade the meat in the mirim, soy sauce, oyster sauce, and salt and pepper. Set aside while you prepare the sauce and vegetables.
3. Prepare the gochujang sauce by mixing all the ingredients together in a bowl and set aside.
4. Slice the onion finely, and slice the carrot and courgette (zucchini) in fine diagonal strips.
5. Set a frying pan over a medium heat and add 2 tbsp of neutral oil.
6. Add the meat and start to fry.
7. When it is about half cooked, after about 5–7 minutes, add the gochujang sauce and cook until the meat is done.
8. Next, add all the vegetables and stir-fry for about 5 minutes, depending on how crunchy or soft you like your vegetables. A bit of crunch is always good with this dish in my opinion!
9. Serve on a plate and sprinkle some sesame seeds over the top.

TIP

Like with a lot of Korean cooking, measurements for the spices and seasonings are guidelines only and you should adjust the amount of spiciness and sweetness to your personal taste.

Cooking time:
2 hours (or slightly longer)

Spiciness:
Mild

GALBI-JJIM

SHORT RIB STEW

Galbi-jjim or short rib stew is one of the most widely-loved Korean national dishes, and it has also stolen the hearts and taste buds of many people the world over. It is a symbol of a special meal, and the mere presence of it on a dinner table will excite any Korean person. When beef short ribs are cooked slowly over two hours in sweet soy sauce, the meat falls off the bone and creates the most delicious dish. This recipe takes time, but the process is not hard and it is well worth the effort. Try this with mashed potato – and you can omit the red chilli if you want it completely mild for small children.

SERVES A FAMILY OF 4

- 1 kg (2 lb 3 oz) beef short ribs
- 300 ml (10 fl oz/2½ cups) water
- 1 large onion, sliced into quarters
- 300–400 g (10½ oz–14 oz) daikon radish (mooli), washed and peeled. Cut into 4-cm (1½-in) thickness tubed then in half into chunky semi-circles
- 3 medium carrots cut into 3–4-cm (1–1½-in) chunks
- 5 spring onions (scallions), cut into 5-cm batons
- 2 fresh red chillies, halved lengthwise

Sauce

- ½ large onion
- 10 cloves garlic
- 1 x 2.5-cm (1-in) piece of ginger
- 150 ml (5 fl oz/generous half cup) soy sauce
- 2 tbsp glucose (corn) syrup or 1 extra tbsp sugar
- 2 tbsp sugar
- 1 tbsp oyster sauce
- 150 ml (5 fl oz) mirim
- ½ tsp Korean black pepper
- 2 tbsp sesame oil
- 1 Korean/Asian pear grated (optional)

METHOD

Note: Most short ribs are usually sold in massive sizes. If you get them from your local butcher, you can ask for them to be cut in half: a width of about 6–7 cm (2–3 in). Otherwise, you can cook them as they are, or cut off the meat and cook without the bones.

1. If you have time, it is best to soak the ribs in cold water for 2–3 hours, or overnight, in a big pot. This will draw all of the excess blood out of the bones.
2. Remove the ribs from the water and cut off all of the visible fatty parts.
3. In a large pan, place the meat into cold water and bring to the boil. Rinse under cold water, rubbing off all the impurities.
4. Place the ribs into a big heavy-bottomed pan while you make the sauce.
5. If you have a food processor or blender, blend all of the sauce ingredients together; otherwise hand grate the pear, onion, garlic and ginger, and mix

with all the wet ingredients.

6. Pour in the sauce over the meat and add the water.
7. Set on a high heat to begin with until everything comes to a boil. Then lower the heat right down and simmer for about 1½–2 hours. Alternatively, you can place the pot in a preheated oven at 160°C (320°F) for 2–2½ hours.
8. Halfway through the cooking time, add the onion, daikon (mooll) and carrots, then mix. Cook for another 30 minutes to 1 hour depending on the progress of the stew.
9. The stew is nearly ready when the meat is falling-off-the-bone tender and the root vegetables are soft.
10. Next, add the spring onion and red chilli and mix well.
11. If the sauce is not thickened enough, simmer for another 10–15 minutes on the hob with the lid off.
12. Serve on a large platter, sprinkling some sesame seeds over the top.

Cooking time: 20 minutes

Spiciness: mild

ROLLED OMELETTE

This is a classic side dish that Korean kids grow up with, and it's the nation's favourite lunch- box filler. Quick to make, high in protein and packed with nutrients, it's also perfect with salad if you are on a low-carb diet. You can also have it with rice and kimchi, and almost any kind of sauce that you might fancy on the day. It's great with mayonnaise, chilli sauce, ketchup and bbq sauce, and also works amazingly well with pesto and a slice of cheese in a sandwich!

SERVES 3–4

5 medium (US large) eggs

½ tsp salt

1 tbsp Yondu

½ carrot, finely diced

2 spring onions (scallions), stalks only, finely chopped

3 tbsp water

Neutral vegetable oil for frying

METHOD

1. Beat the eggs in a large bowl and season with the salt and Yondu.
2. Add the carrot, spring onions (scallions) and water, and mix.
3. Heat a non-stick pan with some neutral oil on a low–medium heat.
4. Pour 3-4 tbsp of the egg mix into the pan and let it spread out to fill the pan.
5. When it looks about 80% cooked through, start rolling up the egg pancake from one end. It's this still uncooked, runny egg that acts as glue and sticks the egg together.
6. Once you have almost completely rolled the egg, push the rolled egg to one side of the pan to create room to add in more egg mix. Add a spoonful of oil again if necessary. This time, when the egg pancake is about 80% cooked, place the rolled egg on top at one end and roll it up in the new pancake.
7. Repeat the process with the rest of the egg mix. Each time you add the egg mix and roll, it will get bigger and bigger. As the egg roll gets larger, try to shape it into a rectangular, not a circular tube. If the roll still feels soft when you have finished all the egg mix, roll it round to cook on all sides for a few more minutes.
8. Move the egg roll onto a chopping board and let it rest a little. The remaining heat will cook the egg completely.
9. Slice in 1.5–2-cm (½–¾-in) widths and place it on a long plate (if you have one) ready to devour.

TIP

You can add any leftover bits from the fridge: courgette, onion, green beans, pepper, mushrooms, tuna, ham, cooked chicken… Everything can work rolled up in egg!

Suitable for:
vegetarian and vegan

Cooking time:
20 minutes

Spiciness:
mild

CUCUMBER SALAD IN SESAME DRESSING

This recipe is so simple, delicious and refreshing! Some people think cucumbers are bland and lack flavour, but they are really versatile and can be adapted to carry many different flavours. This dish can be prepared in about 10 minutes and goes well with so many meals. It's especially popular with children and is a great way to help them develop an appetite for vegetables and salads.

SERVES 2

3 Persian cucumbers or 1 English salad cucumber
1½ tsp sea salt

Seasoning

2 tbsp soy sauce
1 tbsp vinegar
½ tbsp sugar or sweetener of your choice
2 garlic cloves, minced
3 tbsp sesame oil
1 tbsp Yondu
3 tbsp crushed sesame seeds
⅓ tsp salt

METHOD

1. Wash the cucumbers and slice as thinly as possible.
2. Add the salt and mix well. Leave for 10 minutes to release the moisture from the cucumber slices.
3. Squeeze the slices gently with your hands and drain water well.
4. In a mixing bowl, combine all the seasoning ingredients.
5. Add the squeezed cucumber slices and mix well. Serve and enjoy!

TIP

Just add 1 tsp of gochugaru and ½ tbsp of fish sauce to transform this recipe into a spicy cucumber kimchi salad.

Cooking time:
15 minutes (or less)

Spiciness:
medium

SHREDDED DAIKON KIMCHI SALAD

RADISH

If you can find good quality daikon radish (mooli), try making this quick kimchi salad that can be kept in the fridge for up to two weeks. It can be mixed into rice to make bibimbap and goes with most Korean dishes. Adjust the amount of gochugaru (chilli powder) to your preferred spice level, or omit it completely if you want a plainer side salad. This salad goes with almost anything: a refreshing side for steak and chips, grilled chicken, omelette or even as a sandwich filler.

SERVES 3–4

500 g (1 lb 2 oz) daikon radish (mooli)
1 tbsp gochugaru (2 tbsp if you like it extra spicy)
1 tbsp garlic, crushed
2 tbsp Korean plum syrup
2 tbsp fish sauce
1 tbsp salted shrimp
1 tbsp roasted sesame seeds
1½ tbsp sugar
2 tbsp apple vinegar
a few shakes Ajinomoto
½ tsp salt
1–2 small spring onions (scallions), stalks only, roughly chopped
1 tbsp sesame oil

METHOD

1. Wash and peel the radish and slice into thin strips.
2. Place in a large bowl, add the gochugaru and mix well. This will dye the radish red.
3. Next, simply add the remaining ingredients and mix well. Taste, and add a little more salt if it lacks saltiness, more vinegar if you like it more sour, and sugar if you want a 'rounder' taste.
4. This salad can be eaten fresh, but a big batch can be kept in the fridge for up to 2–3 weeks. It will taste better after a day or two when it matures.
5. You can make the simplest, yummiest bibimbap with this radish dish:

   1 bowl of sticky rice
   + 2 sunny side up eggs
   + 2 tbsp of radish kimchi salad
   + 1 tbsp sesame oil
   + 1 tbsp soy sauce
   + little bit of gochujang

Cooking time:
20 minutes (plus additional 30 minutes to simmer)

Spiciness:
mild

BEEF AND SEAWEED BIRTHDAY SOUP

Korean people love giving special meaning to foods: a typical example would be the beef and seaweed birthday soup. As a Korean, it's almost 100 per cent guaranteed that you will end up eating this soup at least once on your birthday.

It is thought to have come from the tradition of new mothers being served seaweed soup daily for the first month, due to seaweed's health benefits; it's rich in protein, fibre, vitamins and antioxidants. This soup symbolizes your family's good wishes for your health and wellbeing. In childhood, your mum serves seaweed soup along with other treats on your birthday, and in your adulthood someone close to you will prepare the soup as a symbol of their love and care for you.

This is often served with a spoonful of rice dropped in and a dollop of kimchi on top.

SERVES 3–4

250 g (9oz) beef (any cut works for this recipe)
15 g (½ oz) dried seaweed
3-4 tbsp sesame oil
3 tbsp soy sauce
1.5 litres (3 pts) water
1 medium white onion, cut into quarters
½ tsp sea salt
1 tbsp fish sauce
½ tsp Dasida stock powder
½ tbsp garlic, minced
¼ tsp black pepper

METHOD

1. Cut the beef into small chunks and set aside.
2. Place the seaweed (available at all Korean or Japanese grocery stores) in a big bowl of water. Once it has softened and expanded, squeeze out the water with your hands. If you have used big pieces of seaweed, cut into small pieces with a pair of scissors. Set aside.
3. Set a heavy saucepan over a medium heat and add the sesame oil.
4. Add the beef and stir-fry until browned.
5. Next, add the soy sauce and stir some more until the meat is cooked through.
6. Now, add the seaweed and keep

stirring. It will soak up all the excess meat juice and soy sauce.

7. Add the water, cover and bring to the boil.
8. Add the onion and season with the salt, fish sauce and Dasida stock powder.
9. Turn the heat to low and simmer gently with the lid on for 30 minutes to 1 hour until everything is nice and soft. If you choose a slightly leaner and tougher cut, simply simmer for extra time until the meat becomes tender.
10. Add the minced garlic and black pepper, stir, taste and adjust the seasoning if necessary. Serve in a bowl, and enjoy.

Cooking time:
15 minutes

Spiciness:
mild

COURGETTE NAMUL

This is a simple, delightfully tasty dish you must try. You can use this as a component of a delicious bibimbap or as a side to a bowl of rice. It is definitely one of the yummiest ways to enjoy courgettes!

SERVES 2–3

- 1 large courgette (zucchini), about 300 g (10½ oz)
- 2 tbsp sesame oil
- 2–3 cloves garlic, crushed or sliced thinly
- 2–3 pinches salt
- ½ tbsp soy sauce
- 1 tsp Yondu
- 1 spring onion (scallion), stalk only
- ½ tbsp fish sauce
- ½ tbsp sesame seeds

METHOD

1. Cut the courgette (zucchini) in half lengthwise, then thinly slice it diagonally into semi-circles.
2. Set a frying pan on a medium heat and add the oil, minced garlic and sliced courgette.
3. Sauté for about 5 minutes until the courgette is softened slightly but retains some crunch.
4. Take off the heat, add the remaining seasonings and let it mix well.
5. Transfer to a serving bowl or plate, sprinkling over the finely chopped spring onion and sesame seeds.

TIP

Add a teaspoon of gochugaru for a dish with a little more kick!

Cooking time:
15 minutes

Spiciness:
mild

STEAMED AUBERGINE NAMUL

If aubergines (eggplants) are your thing, this Korean dish will be a nice change to more common ways of cooking them. Most of the cooking time is for steaming, and the rest is over in minutes! Steaming the aubergines makes them so soft and releases their natural sweetness. The seasoning here is typical of that added to Korean vegetable namul and brings out the best flavours in different vegetables. And if you would like a little something extra, a sprinkling of gochugaru works very well.

SERVES 2–3

- 2 large or 3 small (about 500 g/1 lb 2 oz) aubergine (eggplant)
- 2 spring onions (scallions), stalks only, finely chopped
- ½ tsp salt
- ½ tbsp roasted sesame seeds
- ½ tbsp garlic, crusged
- 1½ tbsp soy sauce
- 1 tbsp sesame oil
- ½ tsp Dasida stock powder
- ⅓ tsp Korean black pepper
- 1 tbsp fish sauce

METHOD

1. Slice the aubergine (eggplant) in half lengthwise, and cut in half widthwise.
2. Place it in a steamer and steam for about 6–7 minutes. If a fork goes in smoothly it is cooked. You can also steam the aubergine in a microwave by wetting the aubergine and cooking for about 4–5 minutes.
3. Let the aubergine cool down a little and then pull by hand into 2-cm wide (1-in) strips in a mixing bowl.
4. Add the remaining ingredients and mix well.
5. Taste, and adjust the saltiness accordingly by adding more salt or soy sauce, depending on your preference.

Cooking time: 1 hour

Spiciness: medium

JAPCHAE WITH PULLED GOCHUJANG CHICKEN

The process of cooking this japchae is pretty much the same as the vegetarian version in Chapter 1. This one has a slight spiciness to it as the chicken is seasoned with gochujang sauce. It can be eaten as a standalone main dish or have it on rice – this is one of the rare occasions that you can put noodles on rice as a topping! And, as with any spicy food, a great accompaniment to tone things down a little would be a gentle soup (such as the birthday soup on page 80).

SERVES A FAMILY OF 4

Follow this guidance loosely. You can use as little or as many vegetables as you want. As long as the noodles are seasoned well, it will taste great either way.

One chicken breast (about 200 g/7 oz)
1 large carrot, julienned
1 small onion, sliced thinly
1 red and 1 orange Romano peppers, sliced thinly
Salt and pepper
Pinch or two of pepper
200 g (7 oz) spinach
1 tbsp sesame oil
½ tbsp soy sauce
250 g (9 oz) japchae noodles
Neutral vegetable oil for frying

Chicken seasoning

1 tbsp gochujang
1 tbsp gochugaru
2 tbsp soy sauce
1 tbsp oyster sauce
2 tbsp sesame oil
½ tbsp garlic, crushed
1 tbsp sugar

Noodle seasoning

½ tsp salt
1 tbsp garlic, crushed
1 tbsp gochugaru
4 tbsp soy sauce
½ tbsp oyster sauce
2 tbsp sugar
1 tbsp corn syrup (you can replace this with ½ extra sugar)
½ tsp Dasida stock powder
4 tbsp sesame oil
½ tsp Korean black pepper

METHOD

1. Boil the chicken breast for 20 minutes. Let it cool, and then pull apart into thin strips and set aside.
2. In a mixing bowl, combine all of the ingredients for the chicken seasoning, add the chicken, then set aside.
3. Sauté the vegetables with a tablespoon of neutral oil in order of hardness: carrots, onions and peppers. Add a little more oil, as you need more with each addition of vegetables. When all are sautéed and softened, season with a few pinches of salt and a little pepper. Add to the mixing bowl with the chicken and set aside to cool down and let the excess moisture evaporate.
4. Meanwhile, blanch the spinach and refresh in cold water. Squeeze out all the water. Season with 1 tbsp of sesame oil, a pinch of salt, ½ tbsp of soy sauce and some black pepper. Add this to the mixing bowl with the chicken and vegetables and we are nearly ready!
5. Fill a wok two-thirds with water and bring to a boil. Add the japchae noodles and cook for 7 minutes before draining and washing under cold water to get rid of any excess starch. Set aside.
6. Prepare the noodle seasoning by mixing all of the ingredients together in a bowl.
7. Return the noodles to the wok, set over a medium heat and pour in the sauce.
8. Mix well until the noodles have absorbed all the sauce and become coloured and seasoned. This process may take about 5 minutes.
9. Time to mix everything! Add the noodles to the mixing bowl with the vegetables and seasoned chicken. Cut the noodles a few times with a pair of kitchen scissors if they are too long and difficult to handle. Mix everything well.
10. Finish off with a drizzle of sesame oil and some sprinkles of sesame seeds before serving. It's best to serve when it's still warm but japchae is often eaten when it's cold too. It can keep in the fridge for about 2 days and makes a great next-day lunch. You can add some chilli sauce when you reheat it and turn it into a spicy topping for a bowl of rice.

TIP

You can adjust the level of spiciness by using less gochujang and gochugaru. If you like it spicier, adding chilli oil is a great option!

Cooking time:
30 minutes

Spiciness:
mild

SEAFOOD PAJEON

KOREAN SEAFOOD PANCAKE

Did I mention that Korean people like having specific foods on special days and events? This one is slightly unique. We eat pancakes on rainy days! It's believed that sizzling pancakes sound like raindrops. I think we just create excuses to eat more! These seafood pancakes are probably one of the dishes at Korean restaurants most frequently ordered by non-Koreans. I have yet to meet anyone who doesn't like them. They make an easy mid-week treat.

MAKES 2 PANCAKES OF 25-CM (10-IN) DIAMETER

150 g (5 oz) fresh or frozen seafood of your choice (prawns, squid or clams are typically used)
6–7 spring onions (scallions) stalks only (about 100 g/3½ oz), sliced in half lengthwise and cut into 4-cm (1½-in) batons.
1 carrot: (about 100 g/3½ oz), julienned
½ onion (about 100 g/3½ oz) sliced finely
½ courgette (zucchini) (about 100 g/3½ oz), julienned
100 g (3½ oz) Chinese chive, washed and cut into batons
1 fresh red chilli (optional), sliced finely

Batter

100 g (3½ oz/scant 1 cup) plain (all-purpose) flour
60 g (2 oz) potato starch
1 tsp baking powder
⅓ tsp salt
½ tsp Dasida stock powder
150 ml (5 fl oz) water

METHOD

1. Defrost the seafood if using frozen, and cut into small pieces, about 2 cm (1 in) in size.
2. Prepare the vegetables and set aside.
3. In a mixing bowl, gently combine all the batter ingredients. Don't worry about any lumpy bits; everything will mix together when you add the vegetables. Overworking the batter makes stodgy pancakes, which you want to avoid. We want airy and crispy pancakes!
4. Add the vegetables and seafood to the batter and turn gently to coat everything evenly. Don't worry if there seems to be almost too many vegetables for the amount of batter. For the Korean pancakes, the batter acts more as a glue to hold the ingredients together rather than to add volume.
5. Heat 3–4 tbsp of neutral oil in a non-stick frying pan on a high heat. You need to almost deep fry the pancake, so use plenty of oil.
6. Spread out the pancake mix as thinly as possible, and move it around from time to time to make sure the oil coats

the entire surface and it cooks evenly.

7. Spread out some red chilli slices evenly on the still wet top side of the pancake.
8. When the bottom is golden brown and crispy, flip and add more oil to cook the other side. Cook until crispy on both sides – it takes around 5 minutes per side – there is no need to flip more than a couple of times.
9. Serve whole or cut into little squares. It is lovely with a classic dipping sauce (pages 62, 112 and 124) or any dip of your choice.

1. BONELESS KOREAN FRIED CHICKEN IN HONEY BUTTER GARLIC GLAZE
2. TRADITIONAL KOREAN FRIED CHICKEN IN YANGNYUM GLAZE
3. CHICKEN DRUMSTICKS IN CHILLI GARLIC SOY GLAZE
4. KOHLRABI PICKLE FOR FRIED CHICKEN V
5. CLASSIC TTEOKBOKKI
6. ROYAL TTEOKBOKKI
7. KOREAN GRILLED PORK DUMPLINGS
8. CLASSIC KIMBAP
9. SPICY CHICKEN KIMBAP WITH LETTUCE AND EGGS
10. KIMCHI PANCAKE V

STREET FOOD, KOREAN-STYLE

The Korean street-food scene is hugely vibrant and really shows our colourful character through food. There are an endless number of outdoor food markets up and down the country, and they are popular tourist attractions. In this chapter, I have selected some of the most loved street foods from Korea that can easily be recreated using common ingredients. Some you may be already familiar with, and some may be new to you, but these are definitely unshifting firm favourites when it comes to casual indulgences in my home country. It's worth noting that you can mix and match the chicken glazes and cuts of chicken to suit your taste.

The recipes in this chapter are great for making gatherings with friends a little more special, and are a fantastic way to kick-start your weekend. Best served with some chilled beers!

Cooking time:
30 minutes

Spiciness:
mild

BONELESS KOREAN FRIED CHICKEN IN HONEY BUTTER GARLIC GLAZE

It is a standing joke that KFC should stand for Korean Fried Chicken because Koreans do fried chicken so well, and the fried-chicken scene in Korea is something you have got to experience once. You would need to stay in Korea for a whole month to try all the different types of fried-chicken dishes Korea has on offer. This recipe gives you a strong, crispy batter that goes well with the buttery, salty glaze. The honey garlic glaze is very popular in Korea but I have not seen it much elsewhere. It has an addictive savoury and sweet taste that keeps you going back for piece after piece. The recipe may seem complicated at first, but the prep really only takes 20 minutes and the frying can be done in 10 minutes. I hope you give it a try!

SERVES 2–3 PEOPLE TO SHARE

Chicken

500 g (1 lb 2 oz) chicken breast or mini fillets
1 tsp salt
½ tsp Korean black pepper
½ tsp ground ginger
½ tsp garlic powder
½ tsp onion powder
½ tsp Korean curry powder (or any curry powder)
Neutral vegetable oil for frying (about 1 litre/2 pts)

Dry seasoned flour

200 g (7 oz/1½ cups) plain (all-purpose) flour
3 tbsp potato starch
1 tbsp salt
2 tsp Korean black pepper
1 tsp garlic powder
1 tsp onion powder

Wet batter

60 g (2 oz/½ cup) plain (all-purpose) flour
1 medium (US large) egg
200 ml (7 fl oz/scant 1 cup) sparkling water

Glaze

60 g (2 oz) butter
2 tbsp garlic, crushed
2 tbsp honey
1 tbsp sugar
3 tbsp soy sauce
2–3 tbsp water
Sprinkle dried parsley to garnish

METHOD

I like to make the glaze before frying the chicken. This way, it has time to cool down and thicken, and it can be brushed onto the chicken just as it comes out of the oil. You can then serve the fried chicken at its prime – crispy and hot!

1. Place all of the ingredients for the glaze in a small pan and set over a medium heat.
2. Bring to a boil, then reduce the heat to low and let thicken for about 5 minutes.
3. Once the liquid has thickened slightly and has a nice shiny gloss, set aside until you are ready to use.
4. Next, prep the chicken. If you are using chicken breasts, slice into strips around 2 cm (¾ in) thick – a chicken goujon size.
5. In a bowl mix the salt, pepper, garlic, ginger and onion powders and Korean curry powder.
6. Drop the chicken pieces into this spice mix and let it season for 10–20 minutes.
7. In a separate bowl, mix all the seasonings for the dry seasoned flour. Add 2 tablespoons of sparkling water and rub into the flour mix, creating 'lumpy' bits that will create a crunch when fried. Repeat this process a few times, adding 2 tablespoons of water each time, until you create enough bits.
8. Take a separate bowl and make the wet batter by mixing together the flour, egg and sparkling water.
9. Coat the chicken lightly in the seasoned flour first, then dip it in the wet batter before dipping once more in the seasoned flour. Lay it flat on a plate to rest while you prepare the remaining chicken strips in the same way.
10. Now you are ready to fry the chicken. Heat up about 1 litre (2 pts) of neutral oil and bring to a temperature of around 170°C (340°F).
11. Fry the chicken pieces for about 4 minutes until they are a light golden brown.
12. Remove and rest while you bring the oil up to 180°C (360°F).
13. Fry the chicken pieces for the second time for about 2 minutes until they are very crispy.
14. When they are ready, you can either toss them in the mixing bowl with the glaze, or use a brush to coat the pieces.

    Sprinkle over some dried parsley before serving and enjoy! A cold glass of beer on the side is a must for Korean fried chicken.

TIP

In Korea, all fried chicken is served with a specific pickle made to accompany fried chicken. This goes great with the kohlrabi pickle on page 106.

Cooking time:
40 minutes

Spiciness:
medium to high

TRADITIONAL KOREAN FRIED CHICKEN IN YANGNYUM GLAZE

Yangnyum glaze is the oldest and most traditional of all the chicken glazes enjoyed in Korea. When I was growing up in Korea in the 80s, fried chicken came in only two varieties: plain or yangnyum. The crunch of the crushed peanuts, spiciness of the gochujang and sweetness of the sugar and corn syrup makes this a taste bomb of a fried chicken.

SERVES 2–3 PEOPLE

Chicken

500 g (1 lb 2 oz) skinless chicken thighs
½ tsp salt
½ tsp Korean black pepper
½ tsp ground ginger
50 g (2 oz/⅓ cup) plain (all-purpose) flour
50 g (2 oz) potato starch
1 tsp baking powder
1 medium (US large) egg
50 ml water (3 tbsp)
700 ml (1½ pts) oil for frying

Glaze

1 tbsp chilli oil
1 tbsp sesame oil
½ white onion (about 100 g/3½ oz), chopped
1 tbsp garlic, roughly crushed or chopped
1 red chilli, roughly chopped
3 tbsp sugar
3 tbsp soy sauce
3 tbsp corn syrup
5 tbsp ketchup
1 tbsp gochujang
½ tbsp gochugaru
50 ml water
Crushed roasted peanuts to garnish

METHOD

1. Start by making the glaze. In a frying pan, add both oils and stir-fry the onion, garlic and chilli on a medium heat until the onion is softened.
2. Add the rest of the glaze ingredients, apart from the crushed peanuts.
3. Stir everything together well until the liquid bubbles up. Lower the heat and let it bubble and thicken.
4. When thickened, turn off the heat and set aside.
5. Now prepare the chicken. Cut the thighs into bite-sized pieces and pat dry. Place in a large bowl.
6. Add the salt, pepper and ginger and leave to marinate for at least 10 minutes. Then add the remaining

ingredients: flour, potato starch, baking powder, egg and water. Mix everything so the chicken pieces are well-coated.

7. Heat the oil to about 170°C (340°F) and fry the chicken pieces for about 4–5 minutes until light brown, then remove.
8. Heat the oil again, this time to 180°C (360°F), and fry the chicken for a second time, for a couple of minutes, until nicely crispened.
9. Remove the chicken from the oil and immediately mix in a large bowl with the glaze. Sprinkle over the crushed peanuts before serving with steamed white rice.

Cooking time: 40 minutes

Spiciness: medium

CHICKEN DRUMSTICKS IN CHILLI GARLIC SOY GLAZE

The last of the fried-chicken recipes in this book is the simplest variation and the one that I go to the most. You can use chicken wings instead of drumsticks, if you prefer. This glaze is savoury, sweet and spicy all at once and has a very addictive taste you will find hard to resist. You can easily adjust the spiciness by varying the amount of chillies you use, or even omit the chilli altogether and let small children enjoy them too.

SERVES 2

Chicken

- 500 g (1 lb 2 oz) chicken drumsticks (usually about 6 smallish drumsticks)
- 1 tsp salt
- ½ tsp Korean black pepper
- ½ tbsp garlic, minced
- 2 red chillies, roughly chopped
- ½ tbsp ginger, minced
- 2 tbsp soy sauce
- 4 tbsp potato starch
- Neutral vegetable oil for frying

Glaze

- 2 tbsp sesame oil
- 4 tbsp soy sauce
- 2 tbsp mirim
- 2 tbsp corn syrup
- 1 tbsp sugar
- ½ oyster sauce
- 1 tbsp garlic, roughly crushed or chopped
- 2 tbsp water
- 2 spring onions (scallions), stalks only, roughly chopped, to garnish

METHOD

1. Start by placing the chicken drumsticks in a freezer bag, and adding the salt, pepper, garlic, chillies, ginger and soy sauce. Leave for 10–30 minutes to marinate while you make the glaze, shaking it from time to time.
2. To make the glaze, add all of the glaze ingredients to a frying pan set over a medium heat.
3. Mix well and bring the liquid up to a boil.
4. Once it bubbles up, lower the heat and let it thicken for a few minutes before removing from heat and setting aside until the chicken is fried.
5. When the chicken has finished marinating in the freezer bag, add the

potato starch and shake well to thinly coat the chicken evenly.

6. Heat the oil to 170°C (340°F) in a large frying pan or a wok. Frying in enough oil makes a good crispy fried chicken and the end result is less greasy.
7. Place the chicken in the oil and leave to fry for about 12–15 minutes on a medium–high heat.
8. Remove the chicken when it's all cooked. If you are happy with the crispiness, you can move straight to glazing. However, if you want it to be extra crispy, fry one more time for a couple of minutes at a slightly higher temperature, about 180°C (350°F).
9. Toss the fried chicken pieces into the glaze and mix well.
10. Transfer to a serving plate and sprinkle finely chopped spring onion.

Suitable for: vegetarian and vegan | **Cooking time:** 10–15 minutes | **Spiciness:** mild

KOHLRABI PICKLE FOR FRIED CHICKEN

Kohlrabi is a great alternative to daikon radish (mooli) for making this pickle for fried chicken. Whenever I can't find good quality daikon radish, I use kohlrabi as they are the closest thing to a radish. In Korea, whenever you order fried chicken, you will get served with these delicious white cubes. This is a type of light pickle that is almost exclusively eaten with fried chicken.
It cleanses your palate when you have greasy food.

SERVES 3–4

3 medium kohlrabi (about 450 g/1 lb)

Pickle brine

200 ml (7 fl oz/scant 1 cup) water
100 ml (3½ fl oz/scant ½ cup) apple cider or white wine vinegar
100 g (3½ oz/scant 1 cup) sugar
½ tbsp salt

METHOD

1. Peel the kohlrabis and cut them into 2 cm x 2-cm (1 in x 1-in) cubes.
2. Put the cubes into a glass jar or a container, leaving enough space for the pickle brine.
3. In a saucepan, add the water, sugar, vinegar and salt, and bring to a boil.
4. Pour the hot brine over the cut kohlrabi.
5. Let it cool down before putting in the fridge.
6. This is best eaten the next day.

TIP

You will be left with a lot of brine when you finish eating the radish cubes. This can be reboiled and used a couple more times.

TIP

Hard-boiled eggs are often added as a topping to this dish. Cut the boiled egg in half and serve on the side. Crumbly egg yolk goes very well mixed with the tteokbokki sauce.

Cooking time:
30 minutes

Spiciness:
high

CLASSIC TTEOKBOKKI

If you asked me what the most common street food in Korea would be, hands down, it would be tteokbokki. This casual, low-cost street food of rice-cake sticks simmered in sauce is always found in little food stalls around school gates all over Korea. In fact, you will be able to find all kinds of tteokbokki varieties at different school gates, with some schools famous for their tteokbokki scene. Korean children of all ages rush with their friends after a long school day and giggle over a hot plate of this fun dish. Tteokbokki is one of everyone's fondest memories of their school days.

SERVES 2–3

300 g (10½ oz) rice cake sticks
2–3 Korean fish cake sheets (depending on taste)
4–5 spring onions (scallions)
500 ml (1 pt/2 cups) water
⅓ tsp salt
½ tbsp garlic, minced

Sauce paste

1½ tbsp gochugaru
2 tbsp gochujang
2 tbsp sugar
1 tbsp corn syrup
2 tbsp soy sauce
1 tbsp oyster sauce
⅔ tsp Dasida stock powder
1 tbsp vegetable oil
½ tsp Korean black pepper

METHOD

1. The fresh soft rice cakes available from bigger Korean stores are the best but a fridge-kept packet is good enough and is superior to the frozen type. If you have bought frozen rice cake sticks, soak them in water to unthaw while you start preparing the other ingredients.
2. Slice the spring onions (scallions) in half lengthwise and then cut them into 5-cm (2-in) batons. Then take the fish cake sheets and cut them into small strips or triangles.
3. In a large frying pan, spread out the spring onions and fish cake sheets, and add the water.
4. Set over a medium heat and add the salt and minced garlic. Cover and bring to a boil.
5. Meanwhile, make the sauce paste by mixing together all of the ingredients in a bowl.
6. When the liquid in the frying pan has come to the boil, lower the heat and add the rice cake sticks and the paste. Stir well and let it all simmer for 5–7 minutes until the rice cake sticks get nicely soft.
7. If the sauce is still too runny, open the lid and let it simmer for a few more minutes to thicken further.

Cooking time: 30 minutes

Spiciness: mild

ROYAL TTEOKBOKKI

This tteokbokki is thought to have received its royal moniker from the 19th-century dish that was developed in the royal palace to be served to the royal family. It features marinated beef and rice cake in a gentle soy sauce. It is sometimes called bulgogi tteokbokki because the meat is marinated in a similar way to making bulgogi. Mild in taste, it is the children's go-to tteokbokki until they can take a spicier heat.

SERVES 2

300 g (10½ oz) rice cake sticks
150 g (5 oz) beef, finely sliced (any steak meat works well)
2–3 shiitake mushrooms, thinly sliced
1 tbsp sesame oil
1 tbsp vegetable oil
⅓ carrot, sliced in half lengthwise then in fine diagonals
⅓ onion, sliced
2 spring onions (scallions), stalks only, cut into 5-cm (2-in) batons
⅓ tsp Dasida stock powder
1 fresh red chilli (optional), thinly sliced lengthwise
½ tbsp sesame seeds

Marinade

2 tbsp soy sauce
½ tbsp sugar
½ tbsp garlic, crushed
½ tsp Dasida stock powder
1 tbsp sesame oil
⅓ tsp Korean black pepper

Rice cake seasoning

1 tbsp soy sauce
½ tbsp sugar
1 tbsp sesame oil

METHOD

1. The fresh soft rice cakes available from bigger Korean stores are the best but a fridge-kept packet is good enough and is superior to the frozen type. If you have bought frozen rice cake sticks, soak them in water to unthaw while you start preparing the other ingredients.
2. If you have bought frozen rice cake sticks, soak them in water to unthaw while you prepare the rest of the dish.
3. When thawed, drain the water and add the rice cake seasoning ingredients. Mix well and set aside.
4. Make the marinade by mixing together all the ingredients in a large bowl.
5. Cut the thinly sliced beef into small pieces and add to the marinade bowl along with the mushrooms. Let them marinate for at least 10 minutes.
6. Set a pan on a medium heat and add the sesame oil and vegetable oil. When hot, add the meat, mushrooms and carrots. Sauté for a few minutes until the meat is cooked. If you like more sauce, add an extra 100 ml (3½ fl oz) of water and 2 tbsp soy sauce and let the sauce simmer a little to thicken.

7. Next, add the rice cake, spring onions (scallions) and onion. Add 3 tbsp of water and cover to steam the ingredients for a few minutes. Remove the lid and continue to stir on a medium-low heat until the vegetables are softened.
8. Add a sprinkle of Dasida stock powder and taste. At this stage you can add a little more salt or soy sauce if needed.
9. If you would like to add a fresh red chilli, do it now and mix into the dish.
10. Transfer to a serving dish and sprinkle over some sesame seeds to finish.

Cooking time:
1 hour

Spiciness:
mild

KOREAN GRILLED PORK DUMPLINGS

This is a classic Korean dumpling recipe with simple ingredients that are readily available outside of Korea. You can make variations of dumplings by using different ingredients, such as prawns and kimchi. I think this version works really well, particularly as it can be cooked in a variety of ways – boiled, steamed or even fried – and can be made in a big batch and frozen for rainy days.

Dumplings are one of my absolute favourite foods. They are nutritionally balanced, delicious pockets of goodness neatly wrapped up in soft edible wrappers. Making a huge batch of about 200 dumplings and freezing them was the last significant act I did before having my babies here in the UK. Being away from family, that was my way of ensuring that I, or my husband, could fix healthy meals quickly and easily.

MAKES 40–50 DUMPLINGS

500 g (1 lb 2 oz) minced pork
4 packets dumpling skins
1 bunch (about 200 g/7 oz) Chinese chives
200 g (7 oz) sweetheart cabbage
300 g (10½ oz) medium hard tofu
Neutral vegetable oil for frying

Seasoning

2 tbsp garlic, crushed
1 tsp ginger, minced
1½ tsp salt
4 tbsp soy sauce
1 tsp Dasida stock powder
2 tbsp mirim
5 tbsp sesame oil
1 tsp Korean black pepper
1 medium (US large) egg

Dipping sauce

2 tbsp soy sauce
½ tbsp vinegar
½ tbsp gochugaru
½ tbsp sesame oil
1 tsp sesame seeds
1 tsp finely chopped spring onion (scallion)

METHOD

Note: You can use any dumpling skins except wonton skins. If you can't find Korean dumpling skins, use Japanese gyoza skins. Korean ones are softer to work with and better for making boiled dumplings in soup. Japanese gyoza skins are harder but easier to handle when shaping and better for grilled dumplings.

1. Dumpling skins are usually sold frozen. Take them out a few hours before

making so they are completely thawed and soft to work with.

2. First, make the dipping sauce by mixing all of the ingredients together in a bowl.
3. Next, prepare the vegetables. Wash and finely slice the Chinese chives, and slice the sweetheart cabbage before chopping into small pieces.
4. In a big mixing bowl, combine the meat, vegetables and tofu with all of the seasoning ingredients. Best to get a pair of kitchen gloves and get your hands in there to combine everything thoroughly. Squash the tofu into a paste with your fingers and mix everything together well. You are now ready to make your dumplings.
5. Get a small bowl of water, which you will use to dab onto the dumpling skin to glue it.
6. Place a dumpling skin on the palm of your non-dominant hand. Using the other hand, dab a fingertip in water and spread a small amount around the edge of the dumpling – only half the circle – closest to you. This is the glue to seal the dumpling.
7. Now place a teaspoonful of the filling in the middle of the skin and fold the skin in half, but not completely. Then, starting from one corner of the skin, start pressing the two skin sides together, pinching together with small folds.
8. Make sure you see no visible gaps or holes when you work your way around to seal the dumpling.
9. Transfer the prepared dumplings to a plate, sitting with their sealed folds facing upwards.
10. To cook the dumplings, heat up a large frying pan with 3 tbsp of neutral oil on a medium heat.
11. Place as many dumplings as will fit comfortably in the frying pan. You will need to do this in batches.
12. Cook the bottom of the dumplings for a few minutes on medium to high heat.
13. When you can hear them sizzling, pour 100 ml (3½ fl oz/scant ½ cup) of water in the pan, cover and lower the heat.
14. Let them steam away for 5–7 minutes. (If cooking from frozen, add a few more minutes to the cooking time.)
15. As all the water evaporates, the bottoms of the dumplings will get nice and crispy. Check periodically so you don't burn them.
16. You should end up with dumplings with crispy browned bottoms and soft steamed tops.
17. Alternatively, you can boil these dumplings for 6–7 minutes and drain and put in a bowl. I like to eat these with a big spoonful of chilli oil. A perfect quick lunch on a cold day!
18. Flip the dumplings upside down when plating them, so the crispy sides face up.
19. Serve with the dipping sauce.

TIP

These dumplings can be added to any noodle soups you are making. They are such a versatile food item to have in your freezer.

Cooking time: 1 hour

Spiciness: mild

CLASSIC KIMBAP

One thing you have to be very careful not to do with kimbap is to call it Korean sushi. Korean people can be rather sensitive about it. The name 'sushi' means 'vinegar rice' in Japanese, as sushi rice is seasoned with vinegar and sugar. Kimbap is a very Korean dish and is always savoury, comprising rice seasoned with salt, sesame oil and sesame seeds. Whereas sushi filling is dominantly raw fish, kimbap can have many varieties of cooked vegetable and meat fillings. Kimbap is a number one picnic dish in Korea, and all Korean children know the excitement of opening a lunch box full of colourful kimbap on school trips. For Koreans, the most typical kimbap roll would consist of three differently-coloured vegetables (orange carrot, green spinach and yellow pickled radish, for example) plus brown beef and yellow egg. In Korea, a bowl of spicy Korean instant ramen, such as shin ramyun, is often ordered together with kimbap. People like to dip the kimbap pieces into the spicy soup.

MAKES 3–4 ROLLS

- A packet of dried seaweed sheets for kimbap/sushi, such as nori
- 600 g (1 lb 5 oz) Korean steamed rice
- 1 pack radish pickle
- 3 medium (US large) eggs
- ½ large cucumber
- 250 g (9 oz) pack spinach
- 1 medium carrot, julienned
- 250 g (9 oz) minced beef or thinly-sliced steak

Rice seasoning

- ½ tsp salt
- 2 tbsp sesame oil
- 1 tbsp sesame seeds
- 1 pack radish pickle

Beef seasoning

- 3 tbsp soy sauce
- ½ tbsp sugar
- 2 pinches salt
- 3 cloves garlic, crushed
- 2 tbsp sesame oil
- Ground black pepper to your taste

TIP

Feel free to follow the recipe loosely and adjust the amount of each ingredient to your taste. You can omit one or two ingredients and it will still taste amazing. Some kimbap features only one or two fillings, but in larger quantities.

PREPARING THE FILLINGS

Prepare all the fillings as follows, season each with a pinch of salt and line them up on a large plate ready to be assembled.

1. **Rice:** Mix the hot steamed rice with the salt, sesame oil and sesame seeds and set aside to cool down. Using it when too hot shrinks the seaweed and makes it soggy, making it impossible to roll properly.
2. **Pickled radish**: These are sold at all Korean stores, pre-prepared and packed neatly for making kimbap at home. Everyone uses store-bought pickles for kimbap making, as they are too time consuming to make from scratch for the small amount you need for kimbap. They can be used straight out of the packet.
3. **Egg sheet:** Beat the eggs with a pinch of salt. Heat a medium frying pan on a low-medium heat with a drizzle of oil. Pour in the beaten eggs and let them cook slowly. When one side is almost cooked, you can turn off the heat and let the residual heat cook the egg sheet through. Move it to a chopping board and let it cool down before slicing it in strips of about 1-cm (½-in) thickness. Slicing the egg sheet very thinly can look nicer when the kimbap is cut and is worth the extra prep time.
4. **Cucumber:** If you are using an English salad cucumber, scrape off the watery seedy part in the middle after slicing the cucumber in half lengthwise. Slice the cucumber halves lengthwise in fine strips. The length of the cucumber should be slightly longer than the rolls themselves.
5. **Spinach:** Place the spinach in a large bowl and pour over some boiling water. Leave for 10 seconds. Refresh under cold water and squeeze in your hands to remove all the water. In a bowl, season with a little salt, sesame oil and soy sauce.
6. **Carrot:** Lightly sauté the julienned carrot with a tablespoon of oil in a frying pan. Season with a little salt. Cook only for a few minutes so it still has a crunch.
7. **Beef:** Marinate the beef in the seasoning, then sauté in a frying pan with a little oil and set aside when cooked.

Continued overleaf

ROLLING THE KIMBAP

1. Lay a sheet of seaweed down on a large chopping board with the rough side facing up.
2. Spread out about 150g of rice as thinly as possible, leaving a 3-cm (1¼-in) gap at the top of the seaweed. This empty gap will act as a seal for the roll. Try to spread out the rice in an even thickness: this is the key to perfect-looking kimbap.
3. Arrange all the fillings in lines on the rice. You only need a small amount of each ingredient. For example, 1–2 lines of radish pickle, 2–3 lines of sliced cucumber and 2 lines of egg. As you get better at rolling, you can increase the amount of each filling.
4. Once everything is lined up, take the end of the seaweed closest to you and lift it up and over, covering the filling.
5. Once you are midway, switch your hand position and use your four fingers to roll and tug in. When you do this, you are trying to push down all the fillings, keeping them all inside and rolling tight. A loose kimbap roll will crumble in pieces when sliced.
6. When you reach the end where you left a gap on the seaweed, hold the roll in place with one hand and dab a few drops of water with a brush on the seaweed, like applying glue.
7. When the water has soaked in a bit, finish rolling and leave it to rest with the connecting part facing down. The weight of the roll will keep the seaweed together until it sticks securely.
8. Brush on a layer of sesame oil on the top half of the roll and slice using a bread knife. If you have a blunt knife you will end up squashing the roll and ruin the hard work.
9. Place the sliced kimbap on a plate and serve with a sprinkle of sesame seeds. Kimbap is usually served without a dipping sauce because it is often accompanied by other foods. But if you'd like to dip, kimchi/sriracha mayo works well.

Cooking time: 1 hour

Spiciness: medium

SPICY CHICKEN KIMBAP WITH LETTUCE AND EGGS

If someone asked me what the best thing about kimbap is, I would definitely say its versatility. There are endless combinations of ingredients you can use to make different kimbap, and you can be as casual or as fancy as you want. Either way, their portability makes them Korea's favourite on-the-go food, and one of the most commonly found street food, along with tteokbokki. By the way, tteokbokki and kimbap are a popular combination, so I recommend you make them together and make a proper meal out of it – dip the kimbap in the sticky tteokbokki sauce!

MAKES 3–4 ROLLS

A packet of dried seaweed sheets for kimbap/sushi, such as nori
600 g (1 lb 5 oz) Korean steamed rice
1 pack radish pickle
3 medium (US large) eggs
½ large salad cucumber
8 leaves baby gem lettuce
250 g (9 oz) chicken thighs, sliced thinly

Rice seasoning

½ tsp salt
2 tbsp sesame oil
1 tbsp sesame seeds

Chicken seasoning

1½ tbsp gochujang
½ tbsp fine gochugaru
1 tbsp soy sauce
½ tbsp sugar
⅓ tsp salt
½ tsp Dasida stock powder
3 cloves garlic, crushed
½ tbsp ground ginger

PREPARING THE FILLINGS

Prepare all the fillings as follows, season each with a pinch of salt and line them up on a large plate ready to be assembled.

1. **Rice:** Mix the hot steamed rice with salt, sesame oil and sesame seeds and set aside to cool down. Using it when too hot shrinks the seaweed and makes it soggy, making it impossible to roll properly.
2. **Pickled radish:** They can be used straight out of the packet.
3. **Egg sheet:** Beat the eggs with a pinch of salt. Heat a large frying pan on a low-medium heat with a spoonful of oil. Pour the beaten eggs and let it cook slowly. When one side is almost cooked, you can turn off the heat and let the residue heat cook the egg sheet through. Move it to a chopping board and let it cool down before slicing it into about 1-cm (½-in) thicknesses.
4. **Cucumber:** If you are using an English salad cucumber, scrape off the watery

seedy part in the middle after slicing the cucumber in half lengthwise. Slice the cucumber halves lengthwise in fine strips. The length of the cucumber should be slightly longer than the rolls themselves.

5. **Chicken:** Mix the chicken seasoning ingredients together in a bowl, add the chicken pieces and marinate for 15–30 minutes. Sauté the marinated meat. Discard any sauce created and just use the dry meat. Use about 50 g (2 oz) per roll.
6. **Lettuce:** Wash and dry before use. We will use 2 baby gem leaves per roll.

ROLLING THE KIMBAP

1. Lay a seaweed sheet down on a large chopping board with the rough side facing up.
2. Spread out about 150g of rice as thinly as possible, leaving a 3-cm (1¼-in) gap at the top of the seaweed. This empty gap will act as a seal for the roll. Try to spread out the rice in an even thickness: this is the key to perfect-looking kimbap.
3. Arrange all the fillings in lines on the rice. You only need a small amount of each ingredient. For example, 1–2 lines of radish pickle, 2–3 lines of sliced cucumber and 2 lines of egg. As you get better at rolling, you can increase the amount of each filling.
4. With this particular kimbap, the lettuce leaves act as an inner wrap that holds all the fillings within them. Place the two lettuce leaves to fill the space on top of the rice and place all the other fillings on it. Roll the lettuce with the filling before you roll the whole thing.
5. Once everything is lined up, take the end of the seaweed closest to you and lift it up and over, covering the filling.
6. Once you are midway, switch your hand position and use your four fingers to roll and tug in. When you do this, you are trying to push down all the fillings, keeping them all inside and rolling tight. A loose kimbap roll will crumble in pieces when sliced.
7. When you reach the end where you left a gap on the seaweed, hold the roll in place with one hand and dab a few drops of water with a brush on the seaweed, like applying glue.
8. When the water has soaked in a bit, finish rolling and leave it to rest with the connecting part facing down. The weight of the roll will keep the seaweed together until it sticks securely.
9. Brush a layer of sesame oil on the top half of the roll and slice using a bread knife. If you have a blunt knife you will end up squashing the roll and ruin the hard work.
10. Place the sliced kimbap on a plate and serve with a sprinkle of sesame seeds.

TIP

You can omit the cucumber and increase the egg. The spicy chicken and creamy eggs mixed with rice are a match made in heaven.

PEACH

Cooking time: 20 minutes

Spiciness: medium

KIMCHI PANCAKE

This is a simple savoury Korean pancake recipe using kimchi. The tanginess of the kimchi mixed with the pancake batter creates a satisfying savoury chew, and the crunchiness of the kimchi pieces adds texture. Feel free to add some protein to this pancake recipe, such as bacon pieces, tuna or minced chicken. And you can adjust the spiciness by adding more kimchi juice and/or fine gochugaru powder when mixing the batter.

SERVES 2–3

350 g (12 oz) kimchi (any Korean shop-bought brand will do)
4 tbsp kimchi juice
3–4 spring onions (scallions), stalks only, sliced diagonally
150 g (5 oz) plain (all-purpose) flour
70 g (3 oz) potato starch
2 tsp baking powder
160 ml (5½ fl oz/⅔ cup) water
1 tsp Dasida stock powder
½ tbsp fine gochugaru
Neutral vegetable oil for frying

Dipping sauce

2 tbsp soy sauce
½ tbsp vinegar
1 red chilli, finely chopped
½ tbsp sesame oil
1 tsp sesame seeds

METHOD

1. Cut the kimchi into 1-cm (½-in) slices and place in a mixing bowl.
2. Add the kimchi juice and the spring onions (scallions).
3. Add all the remaining ingredients and mix gently into a batter, taking care to avoid over-mixing as this makes for stodgy pancakes.
4. In a large frying pan, add a generous amount of neutral oil and place about 3 tbsp of the batter to make small, thin pancakes of about 10 cm (4 in) in diameter.
5. Cook on both sides until they are golden brown and crispy. Add more oil if necessary.
6. Place them on a serving plate and serve with the dipping sauce, which you make by just mixing all the ingredients together. This is often served with a cold beer!

TIP
If you decide to add protein to this recipe, simply mix your choice of protein to the batter and add extra kimchi brine or salt to season. Bacon strips, a can of tuna or a handful of minced chicken all work well.

1. **BIBIM GUKSU** KOREAN COLD NOODLES IN SPICY SAUCE
2. **THREE-COLOUR BOWL WITH EGGS, GOCHUJANG TUNA AND SUGAR SNAPS**
3. **GOCHUJANG AND PAPRIKA SALMON CUBES WITH TENDERSTEM BROCCOLI**
4. **KIMCHI UDON SOUP**
5. **KIMCHI FRIED RICE WITH BACON**
6. **KOREAN BBQ PORK WITH SPICY CUCUMBER SALAD**
7. **KOREAN OMELETTE WITH GARLIC PRAWNS ON RICE**
8. **SPICY BRAISED MACKEREL**
9. **SPICY CHICKEN SKEWERS WITH BROCCOLI IN SESAME DRESSING**
10. **STIR-FRIED KIMCHI AND PORK**

ONE-PLATE MEALS

Korean people love to have a big spread whenever we can, but this is not always practical. Fortunately there are many tasty and nutritionally balanced one-plate, or one-bowl, quick meals that we make. I have selected ten of my favourites that can become your go-to, simple, quick mid-week meals, most whipped up in less than 30 minutes. Protein-rich and nutritious, they can also be batch-cooked for the week ahead. These dishes can be made even healthier with the addition of any simple steamed vegetables.

You can always add a simple soup to go with these meals and, of course, kimchi will always complement these dishes perfectly, too.

Cooking time:
15 minutes

Spiciness:
high

BIBIM GUKSU

KOREAN COLD NOODLES IN SPICY SAUCE

Cold noodles are probably a type of food that most Korean food newbies find difficult to get used to. However, they are very much loved in Korea, especially in the summertime, and they don't get soggy as quickly as hot noodles, which is a plus. This Bibim guksu can be a refreshing summer lunch or served as a side at a big barbeque party to cleanse your palate.

SERVES 2

- 2 medium (US large) eggs, boiled
- 200 g (7 oz) somyun noodles (fine dried Korean noodles)
- ½ cucumber, julienned
- ½ carrot, julienned
- 2 spring onions (scallions), stalks only, finely chopped
- Sesame seeds to garnish

Sauce

- 1 tbsp gochujang
- ½ tbsp fine gochugaru (or more if you like things spicy)
- 1 tbsp sugar
- 1 tbsp Korean plum syrup (can be replaced with a spoonful of marmalade)
- 2 tbsp soy sauce
- 2 tbsp vinegar
- 2 tbsp sesame oil
- ½ tbsp oyster sauce
- ½ tbsp garlic, minced

METHOD

1. First, boil the eggs. I like my eggs a bit runny, but hard-boiled is perfect for this dish. When ready, cool them in cold water, remove the shells and set aside.
2. Fill a pan with water and put on to boil for the noodles. The trick to good elastic noodles is to use a large pot with plenty of water. While waiting for the water to boil, prepare the sauce.
3. Add all of the sauce ingredients to a large bowl and mix well. Taste and adjust the sweetness or spiciness to suit.
4. When the noodle water comes to a boil, cook the noodles for 3 minutes. They cook very quickly, so set a timer.
5. When done, run the noodles under cold water until they have cooled. Drain well.
6. Add the noodles to the bowl with the sauce, and mix to coat well before transferring them to two ramen or pasta bowls.
7. Finally, add the cucumber and carrot toppings along with two boiled egg halves per bowl, and finish off with a sprinkle of sesame seeds and spring onions before serving.

TIP

A lot of people like to increase the sweet and sour flavours of this dish by adding more sugar and vinegar.

Cooking time:
30 minutes

Spiciness:
medium

THREE-COLOUR BOWL WITH EGG, GOCHUJANG TUNA AND SUGAR SNAPS

This three-colour, one-bowl meal features yellow for the eggs, red for the gochujang tuna and green for the sugar snap peas. Feel free to create your own three colours with different ingredients you have at home. As people are more aware of the importance of eating a balanced diet, making sure your meal is not just one colour is a good hack to ensure you are eating well, even with a quick simple meal like this one.

SERVES 2

Eggs

4 medium (US large) eggs
⅓ tsp salt
1 tbsp mayonnaise
½ tbsp oyster sauce
Few shakes Korean black pepper
Few shakes Ajinomoto
Neutral vegetable oil for frying

Gochugang tuna

2 x cans tuna
1 tbsp gochujang
1 tbsp Japanese miso paste
2 tbsp mayonnaise
2 spring onions (scallions), stalks only, finely chopped
1 tbsp corn syrup
1 tbsp soy sauce
2 tsp fine gochugaru
1 tbsp sesame seeds
100 g (3½ oz) sugar snap peas
400 g (14 oz) Korean steamed rice

METHOD

1. Beat the eggs and add the salt and mayonnaise, oyster sauce, black pepper and Ajinomoto, mixing well.
2. Heat a small frying pan with some oil on a medium heat and pour in the egg mix.
3. Scramble the eggs and set aside.
4. Next, drain the tuna and place it into a mixing bowl.
5. Add the other ingredients and mix well.
6. Sauté in a frying pan to evaporate all the moisture off the tuna and set aside.
7. Meanwhile, steam or boil the sugar snaps. Some crunch is always good so I recommend boiling for about 3 minutes and refreshing under cold water.
8. To assemble, put a bed of rice at the bottom of your favourite ramen or pasta bowls. Place the eggs on one half of bowl, the gochujang tuna on the other, and the sugar snaps wherever you like in the bowls.

Cooking time: 40 minutes

Spiciness: medium

GOCHUJANG AND PAPRIKA SALMON CUBES WITH TENDERSTEM BROCCOLI

Salmon is one of the most versatile and approachable fish, and its buttery flesh goes really well with paprika and a hint of gochujang. If you are stuck in a rut of cooking salmon just one or two ways and want to try something different, this recipe may pleasantly surprise you. It's very simple to make and mild enough for children to try.

SERVES 2

- 2 salmon fillets (about 250 g/9 oz), skin removed and cut into chunks
- 400 g (14 oz) Korean steamed rice
- 150 g (5 oz) tenderstem broccoli
- 1 small spring onion (scallion) chopped finely
- Sesame seeds for garnish

Salmon marinade

- 1 tbsp gochujang
- 1 tbsp paprika
- 2 tbsp mayonnaise
- 1 tbsp soy sauce
- 3 tbsp honey
- ½ tsp salt
- 3 tbsp breadcrumbs
- ½ tsp Asian chicken stock powder
- ⅓ tsp black pepper

METHOD

1. In a mixing bowl, make a paste with all the marinade ingredients.
2. Add the salmon cubes and stir until they are well-coated.
3. Leave for 5 minutes to marinate while you preheat the oven to 180°C (360°F).
4. Place the salmon on a flat oven tray and cook for about about 20 minutes.
5. Hopefully you will see the sizzle of the sauce on the surface of the salmon and even some glaze forming from the honey or sugar.
6. Meanwhile, boil the broccoli in some salted water to your preferred texture.
7. Serve the salmon pieces on a plate with some rice and the broccoli, sprinkling some chopped spring onions and sesame seeds over before serving.

TIP
Replace the fish cake with chicken, prawns or the dumplings from page 112 to whip up a hearty protein-rich bowl of udon.

Cooking time:
15 minutes

Spiciness:
medium to high

KIMCHI UDON SOUP

I would like to introduce you to a bowl that will warm you inside out on a cold day. Udon is a versatile noodle that works well in a soup or a stir-fry. Kimchi udon is commonly eaten in Korea as an alternative to the milder Japanese-style udon. This takes as little time to cook as instant noodles but will charge your battery to the full in an ultimately comforting way.

SERVES 1

- 600 ml (1 pt/2½ cups) water
- 100 g (3½ oz) kimchi, with some kimchi juice
- 4–5 tbsp tsuyu (Japanese seasoned soy sauce)
- Salt, to taste
- 1 tbsp fish sauce
- 1 tbsp Dasida stock powder
- 1 tsp fine gochugaru
- 2–3 baby sweetcorn
- 1 portion frozen sanuki udon noodles (they usually come in a pack of 4 individual portions)
- 1 Korean fried fish cake sheet, defrosted and cut into strips
- 2 spring onions (scallions), stalks only, sliced diagonally in 3-cm (1¼-in) batons.
- ½ tsp Korean black pepper
- 1 fresh red chilli, thinly sliced diagonally

METHOD

1. Boil the water in a large pan.
2. Add the kimchi (cut into smaller pieces if needed), tsuyu, salt, fish sauce, Dasida and gochugaru to make the soup base.
3. Add the baby sweetcorn and the udon noodles and boil altogether for about 3 minutes.
4. Add the sliced fish cake sheet and boil everything for another 2 minutes.
5. Add the spring onions (scallions), black pepper and red chilli before turning off the heat.
6. Have a taste, and if it's too salty, add a little water; if under seasoned, add some more salt.
7. Pour into a nice thick bowl to keep it piping hot as long as possible.

TIP
You can use any protein of your choice. Canned tuna makes a great combo with the kimchi, and frankfurters sliced into small pieces work well too.

Cooking time:
30 minutes

Spiciness:
medium to high

KIMCHI FRIED RICE WITH BACON

This iconic dish is one of many things you can cook using mature kimchi that is too strong to eat neat. Cooking the kimchi creates a lovely unique savoury flavour. To minimize mess, I suggest putting the kimchi in a cup or a deep bowl and using kitchen scissors to cut it up. Cooked kimchi goes beautifully with fatty meat like pork, which is why it is common to use pork belly or bacon when making kimchi fried rice.

SERVES 2

- 200 g (7 oz) mature kimchi, cut into small pieces
- 2 tbsp vegetable oil
- 2 tbsp sesame oil
- 3 spring onions (scallions), stalks only, roughly chopped
- 3–4 rashers bacon (about 80 g/3 oz) sliced into bite-sized pieces
- ½ tbsp sugar
- ½ tbsp fine gochugaru
- 400 g (14 oz) Korean steamed rice, cooled
- 1 tbsp soy sauce
- 1 tsp Dasida stock powder
- ½ tsp Korean black pepper
- ½ tbsp fish sauce
- 2 medium (US large) eggs
- Handful roasted seasoned seaweed, crumbled, to serve

METHOD

1. Take a wok or large frying pan and heat the vegetable and sesame oils.
2. When the oil is hot, add the spring onion and stir-fry for a minute. Then add the bacon, followed by the kimchi, sugar and fine gochugaru, stirring all the time to infuse the flavours together. If you like spice, you can increase the amount of gochugaru or add some kimchi juice for more fire.
3. Next, add the rice and mix well with the ingredients. This stage may take a little time. Use two wooden spatulas to mix thoroughly.
4. Add the rest of the seasoning – the soy sauce, Dasida stock powder, black pepper and fish sauce – and mix again.
5. While the fried rice is cooking, in a separate pan, make two soft-fried eggs, one per person.
6. If you are a cheese lover, sprinkle some grated cheese over the rice at the last stage of cooking and let it melt in. This has become a very popular way people eat kimchi fried rice in Korea.
7. When the eggs are cooked, divide the rice between two plates or bowls and serve with the fried egg on top, sprinkling some roasted seaweed over the dish as a finishing touch.

Cooking time:
40 minutes

Spiciness:
mild to medium

KOREAN BBQ PORK WITH SPICY CUCUMBER SALAD

Another classic Korean flavour bomb on a simple, unassuming plate. The sweet soy sauce-marinated grilled pork on steamed rice tastes even sweeter with this spicy tangy cucumber salad on the side. This is a Korean comfort food at its best.

SERVES 2

400 g (14 oz) pork shoulder, thinly sliced against the grain
1 tbsp mirim
1 tbsp soy sauce
½ tbsp oyster sauce
3 tbsp potato starch
3–4 tbsp vegetable oil for frying
Salt and pepper to season the meat
½ white onion, thickly sliced
2 dried Thai red chillies
400 g (14 oz) Korean steamed rice

Sauce

2 tbsp soy sauce
1 tbsp sugar
1 tbsp corn syrup
1 tbsp garlic, crushed
1 tbsp ginger, minced
2 spring onions (scallions), stalks only, finely chopped
½ tsp Korean black pepper
1 tbsp water

Cucumber salad

1 large salad cucumber
½ tbsp soy sauce
⅓ tsp salt
1 tbsp gochugaru
½ tbsp garlic, minced
½ tbsp vinegar
1 tbsp Korean plum syrup
½ tbsp sugar
½ tbsp fish sauce
1 tbsp sesame oil
½ tbsp sesame seeds

METHOD

1. Marinate the pork in the mirim, soy sauce, oyster sauce and a few pinches of salt and black pepper. Set aside for at least 10 minutes.
2. Slice the cucumber in half lengthwise and scrape out the seedy inside. Then slice again, diagonally in fine strips.
3. Next, make the salad dressing by combining all the ingredients together in a bowl. Set aside.
4. Place the potato starch in a bowl and add the marinated pork, coating it thinly.
5. Heat a frying pan with the vegetable oil and add the pork. Fry the pork on both sides on a medium-high heat. When the meat is cooked it should end up with a nice crispy coating. Remove from the pan and set aside.

6. Mix the ingredients for the sauce.
7. In the same pan, add a drizzle of oil then the sliced onion and sauté. Pour in the sauce and dried Thai chillies, and bring it to a boil.
8. Put the cooked meat back into the pan along with the sauce and stir well.
9. Let the sauce reduce slightly while you make the salad by mixing the cucumber slices together with the dressing.
10. Serve the meat on a bed of steamed sticky rice with a generous helping of cucumber salad on the side.

Cooking time:
20 minutes

Spiciness:
mild

KOREAN OMELETTE WITH GARLIC PRAWNS ON RICE

This dish has everything a Korean person loves in a bowl; eggs, rice and garlicky prawns. It is soft, fluffy and gooey, and the ultimate comfort food that requires nothing but a spoon. It's very quick and easy to cook, but manages to feel indulgent, especially if you have treated yourself to some top-quality large prawns.

SERVES 1

6 large or 10 small frozen prawns (shrimp)
3 medium (US large) eggs
2 tbsp vegetable oil
½ tbsp garlic, crushed
1 tbsp mirim
1 tsp oyster sauce
2 tbsp grated mozzarella (optional)
200 g (7 oz) steamed rice
1 tbsp sesame oil
2 spring onions (scallions), stalks only, finely chopped
Salt and pepper for seasoning
1 tsp sesame seeds

METHOD

1. Defrost the prawns.
2. Beat the eggs with a little salt and pepper.
3. Heat a small pan with the vegetable oil on a medium-low heat and add the crushed garlic.
4. Let it sizzle for a minute before adding the prawns, mirim and oyster sauce.
5. Stir-fry for 2–3 minutes until the prawns are almost cooked.
6. Add the beaten eggs and grated mozzarella, if using.
7. Rather than stirring or scrambling the egg, just move the spatula from one side to the other side of the pan, letting the runny egg mix fill the space the spatula creates when it moves. Do this process very gently and slowly, keeping the eggs moist and soft.
8. With the top of the omelette still slightly moist and runny, turn off the heat and place it on a bed of steamed rice.
9. Drizzle sesame oil on top and sprinkle over the finely chopped spring onion, some black pepper and the sesame seeds before serving.

TIP

If you like a little heat, drizzle some chilli oil over the top of your omelette.

Cooking time: 40 minutes

Spiciness: medium to high

KOREAN BRAISED MACKEREL

This is one of the favourite ways Koreans like to cook mackerel. Mackerel's rich taste marries so well with the spicy seasoning in this recipe and creates an umami bomb of a fish stew. It might remind you of some Indian fish curries, but the taste is distinctly Korean. The juices from this dish will make you reach out for more and more rice.

SERVES 2

2 whole mackerel (ask your fishmonger to gut and de-head the fish and slice into 3 or 4 chunky pieces)
¼ daikon radish (mooli) (about 250 g/9 oz)
½ white onion, sliced
250 ml (9 fl oz/1 cup) water
2 fresh red chillies, finely sliced
2 spring onions (scallions), stalks only, diagonally sliced

Sauce

1 tbsp garlic, crushed
1 tbsp gochugaru
1 tbsp gochujang
4 tbsp soy sauce
2 tbsp sugar
1 tbsp fish sauce
1 tsp ginger, grated
½ tsp Korean black pepper
½ tsp Dasida stock powder

METHOD

1. Wash the mackerel pieces under running water and set aside.
2. Wash and peel the daikon radish (mooli) and halve lengthways before slicing into semi-circular pieces.
3. Place the daikon and sliced onion in a heavy-bottomed pot. Pour in just enough water to cover the daikon.
5. Bring to the boil on a medium heat with the lid on and cook for about 5 minutes to soften the vegetable.
6. While the daikon is cooking, take a bowl and mix together all of the sauce ingredients and set aside.
7. When the daikon is soft, place the mackerel pieces on the top and pour the sauce over the fish.
8. Close the lid and let it all simmer for 10–15 minutes, stirring every few minutes to spread the sauce over the fish and help soak in the flavour.
9. When the fish is cooked through, sprinkle the red chilli and spring onion (scallion) slices in and let it cook with the lid on for a few more minutes.
10. Serve with steamed rice and enjoy!

TIP

Quick-boiled bok choy goes really well with this dish. It calms the spiciness and cleanses the palate between mouthfuls of the tangy fishy sauce.

Cooking time: 30 minutes

Spiciness: medium to high

SPICY CHICKEN SKEWERS WITH BROCCOLI IN SESAME DRESSING

Marinated in gochujang sauce and grilled until golden and caramelized, these chicken skewers hit every note: sweet, spicy, savoury. Serve on sticks with rice or lettuce wraps... delicious!

MAKES 6–7 SKEWERS

400 g (14 oz) chicken thighs, skin-on or skinless, depending on your preference
4–5 spring onions (scallions), stalks only, cut into 3-cm (1½-in) batons
250 g (9 oz) broccoli
Salt and pepper

Glaze

1 tbsp soy sauce
1½ tbsp gochujang
1 tbsp corn syrup
1 tbsp sugar
1 tbsp garlic, crushed
1 tbsp mirim

Sesame dressing

5 tbsp sesame seeds, ground
⅓ tsp salt
4 tbsp mayonnaise
½ tbsp apple cider vinegar
½ tbsp lemon juice
1 tsp sugar
1 tbsp soy sauce
Sprinkle of Asian chicken stock powder or Ajinomoto (Japanese umami seasoning)

METHOD

1. Make the sesame dressing by mixing together all the ingredients in a bowl.
2. Cut the chicken into bite-sized pieces. Season with salt and pepper and set aside for about 20 minutes.
3. Meanwhile, slice the spring onions and make the chicken glaze by mixing all the ingredients together in a large bowl.
4. Start making your skewers, alternating pieces of chicken and spring onion.
5. Heat a frying pan on medium-high with a drizzle of neutral oil.
6. Fry the skewers on both sides.
7. When the meat is halfway cooked start brushing the glaze onto the skewers.
8. Brush both sides multiple times while cooking, until the chicken is cooked through and the glaze has reduced and is sticky.
9. Meanwhile, boil the broccoli for 4–5 minutes until tender, then refresh under cold water and pat dry.
10. When the chicken is cooked, place the skewers on a bed of rice, toss the broccoli in the dressing and serve.

Cooking time:
30 minutes

Spiciness:
medium

STIR-FRIED KIMCHI AND PORK

Have I mentioned that pork and kimchi always go hand in hand in Korea? There are so many kimchi and pork combos, and it only takes tasting one of them to know why. The tanginess of the kimchi infused with the fat released from pork creates a type of umami that is hard to resist.

SERVES 2

300 g (10½ oz) pork belly or shoulder, thinly sliced
⅓ white onion, sliced thickly
½ courgette (zucchini) (about 80 g/3 oz)
3 spring onions (scallions), stalks only
200 g (7 oz) mature kimchi, cut into about 3–4-cm (1½-in) pieces.
2 tbsp sesame oil, for frying
1–2 fresh red chillies, depending on your taste, sliced thinly and diagonally
400 g (14 oz) Korean steamed rice

Pork marinade

2–3 pinches salt
½ tbsp garlic, crushed
½ tsp ground ginger
1 tbsp sugar
½ tbsp mirim
2 tbsp soy sauce
1 tbsp gochujang
½ tsp Korean black pepper

Stir-fry seasoning

½ tbsp sugar
2 tbsp sesame oil
½ tbsp oyster sauce
½ tbsp soy sauce
1 tbsp gochugaru
1 tbsp gochujang

METHOD

1. Mix the pork marinade ingredients together in a bowl, then marinate the thinly sliced pork for at least 15 minutes.
2. Slice the onion and cut the spring onion (scallion) stalks diagonally into batons. Cut the courgette (zucchini) in half lengthways and then finely slice into diagonal strips.
3. In a wok or frying pan, add the sesame oil to heat up before adding the marinated pork.
4. Stir-fry the meat for around 5 minutes until it is half-cooked, then add the kimchi and all of the seasoning ingredients.
5. Finally, add the chopped vegetables and stir-fry for a few minutes until the vegetables are cooked but still slightly crunchy. Add the chillies just before serving to heat through.
6. Place on a bed of rice and enjoy!

1. KIMCHI MAC AND CHEESE
2. TUNA AND CUCUMBER FOLDING POCKET KIMBAP
3. BULGOGI AND CHEESE LOADED FRIES
4. CREAMY GOCHUJANG PASTA WITH PRAWNS
5. GOCHUJANG CHEESE AND COURGETTE STUFFED CHICKEN
6. HAM AND CHEESE TOASTIES WITH KIMCHI
7. KIMCHI, CHEESE AND PRAWN FRITTERS WITH SWEETCORN
8. BREAKFAST ROLL KIMBAP
9. ROLLED EGGS WITH HAM AND SEAWEED
10. KOREAN BBQ PULLED PORK SANDWICH WITH QUICK KIMCHI

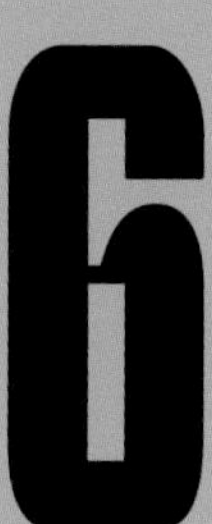

FUSION FLAVOURS: KOREA MEETS THE WEST

For the longest time, I had a mental block when it came to foods presented as fusion cuisine. Foods described this way used to ring alarm bells and raise my suspicions. However, I must give credit to the many dishes out there that have really captured the best of both worlds. Kimchi seems to have landed on the international food scene in a big way in recent years, and people have noticed how well it works with so many 'Western' ingredients, one of which is cheese!

In this chapter, I have chosen some of the classic, well-known Korea-meets-West dishes, as well as recipes that I have developed in my own kitchen with influences from my 30 years of living in multinational environments. I hope you too will continue to experiment in your own kitchen to expand the menu!

Cooking time: 20–30 minutes

Spiciness: mild to medium

KIMCHI MAC AND CHEESE

Another kimchi and cheese combo that works wonders is this kimchi mac and cheese. There is not much to add other than to say that this takes an already iconic dish to a different level!

SERVES 3–4

- 250 g (9 oz) macaroni pasta
- 4 tbsp unsalted butter
- 300 g (10½ oz) cabbage kimchi, chopped small
- 2 tbsp gochujang
- 100 ml (3½ fl oz/scant ½ cup) kimchi juice
- 100 ml (3½ fl oz/scant ½ cup) chicken stock
- 60 grams (2 oz/½ cup) plain (all-purpose) flour
- 400 ml (14 fl oz/1¾ cups) whole milk
- 1 tsp salt
- 150 g (5 oz/1 cup) grated gruyere cheese
- 150 g (5 oz/1 cup) grated mozzarella cheese
- 40 g (1½ oz) breadcrumbs
- 2 spring onions (scallions), roughly chopped

METHOD

1. Cook the pasta in salted water for 9 minutes until al dente. Drain and toss with 2 tbsp of the butter until melted. Place in a large, deep baking tray.
2. Preheat the oven to 180°C (350°F).
3. Add the rest of the butter to a non-stick pan, set over a medium heat and add the chopped kimchi and gochujang. Stir everything up and cook for 5 minutes.
4. Add the kimchi juice and chicken stock and simmer for a few more minutes.
5. Add the flour and mix well, then slowly add the milk while stirring until the mixture is lump-free.
6. Add the salt and keep stirring for about 5 more minutes until the sauce thickens.
7. Remove from the heat, add the cheeses and stir well to get everything combined.
8. Pour the cheese sauce over the macaroni in the baking tray and mix well.
9. Sprinkle with breadcrumbs and bake in the oven for 20–25 minutes until the top is golden brown.
10. Serve in bowls, sprinkled with some spring onions (scallions).

Cooking time:
15 minutes

Spiciness:
Mild

TUNA AND CUCUMBER FOLDING POCKET KIMBAP

These folding pocket kimbap went viral a few years ago and everyone was making kimbap in this way for a while. As everyone knows, tuna and cucumber is a well-loved sandwich filler in many places. The combination works amazingly well with rice too and is a common kimbap filer in Korea. If you find rolling a kimbap a little daunting, this could be a good place to start.

MAKES 2 ROLLS

200 g (7 oz) steamed sticky rice
Salt and pepper to taste
2 tbsp sesame oil
2 sheets seaweed for kimbap/sushi
⅓ salad cucumber, thinly sliced
2 large/4 small lettuce leaves
25 grams sliced cheddar

Tuna filling

1 can tuna
2 tbsp soy sauce
3 tbsp mayonnaise
1 tsp Dijon mustard
½ tbsp lemon juice
⅓ tsp salt
Korean black pepper
1 spring onion (scallion), stalk only, finely chopped
⅓ red onion, finely chopped

METHOD

1. Start by seasoning the steamed rice with salt, pepper and the sesame oil. Set aside to cool.
2. Make the tuna filling by mixing together all the ingredients in a bowl.
3. Lay a sheet of seaweed on a flat surface. Cut the seaweed with a pair of kitchen scissors in the middle up to halfway. Imagine the seaweed is made of four squares and position it with the slit closest to you.
4. Spread half the rice in one square, leaving some space around the edge.
5. Place about 2 tbsp of the tuna filling on the next square of the seaweed and press down slightly to create another circle shape, again leaving some space around the edge.
6. On the next square, place the lettuce and cucumber slices
7. On the last square, place the sliced cheese.
8. Starting from the left side of the slit, start folding one square of the seaweed over the next. And repeat until you end up with a lovely square pocket sandwich made with seaweed.
9. Repeat with the second sheet of seaweed and the remainder of the fillings and enjoy!

Cooking time: 30 minutes

Spiciness: medium

BULGOGI AND CHEESE LOADED FRIES

If you are a fan of loaded fries, this version may just become your favourite. It is savoury, cheesy and tangy all at once, on crispy fries. It's such an indulgent dish, where the fries soak up all the goodness for a sensational flavour hit. Ideal for a Friday treat, after a long week of work, when you let your hair down and munch on a bowl of these fries in front of a movie.

SERVES 3–4

Bulgogi

- 200 g (7 oz) sirloin steak, thinly sliced
- ½ white onion, thinly sliced
- 3 tbsp soy sauce
- 2 tbsp sesame oil
- Pinch salt
- ½ tbsp garlic, crushed
- ½ tbsp sugar
- ½ tbsp Worcestershire sauce

Gochujang mayo sauce

- ½ tbsp gochujang
- 4 tbsp mayonnaise
- 1 clove garlic, minced
- ½ tsp brown sugar
- 2–3 pinches salt
- ½ tbsp lemon juice

Fries and toppings

- About 400 g (14 oz) oven fries
- 100 g (3½ oz) mix of grated mozzarella and cheddar cheese
- 100 g (3½ oz) kimchi, roughly chopped (optional)
- 2 spring onions (scallions), stalks only, thinly sliced

METHOD

1. Marinate the beef in the bulgogi ingredients listed. Try to let it marinate for at least 30 minutes, but it's much better if you can leave it for a few hours.
2. Heat the oven according to the fries' instructions and start cooking them.
3. Make the gochujang sauce by mixing the ingredients together in a bowl. Increase or decrease the proportions according to your taste. Set aside.
4. Next, in a small frying pan, sauté the marinated beef for a few minutes. It should be cooked within 5 minutes. If you want to reduce the rather runny sauce to thicken it, remove the meat and continue to reduce.
5. When the fries are done, place them on a deep plate, sprinkle over the cheese and scatter the bulgogi on top.
6. Put the plate under a grill for a few minutes to melt the cheese.
7. When melted, remove from the grill and scatter kimchi over the top, if wanted.
8. Finally, drizzle the gochujang mayo sauce all over, sprinkle on some spring onions (scallions) and serve.

Cooking time:
20 minutes

Spiciness:
medium to high

CREAMY GOCHUJANG PASTA WITH PRAWNS

The reason why gochujang is used in so many dishes, and why it can be adapted into so many recipes seamlessly, I think, is because of its perfect consistency. This thick chilli condiment can be added to so many things, lending them its unique smoky, spicy chilli flavours. If you are a pasta lover and make pasta multiple times every week, but are a little bored of the same flavours, give this one a try! This will satisfy your craving for a creamy, savoury pasta dish.

SERVES 2

200 g (7 oz) any dried pasta (rigatoni is my favourite)
2 tbsp olive oil
6 cloves garlic, sliced
2 tbsp gochujang
250 ml (8½ fl oz/1 cup) double (heavy) cream
200 g (7 oz) prawns (shrimp) (defrosted weight if using frozen)
1 tbsp butter
25 g (1 oz/¼ cup) Parmesan cheese, grated, plus extra to serve
1 bundle chives or Italian parsley to serve

METHOD

1. Cook the pasta al dente by cooking it 1 minute shy of the time specified on the packet.
2. While the pasta is boiling, start making the sauce.
3. In a large pan, add the olive oil and sauté the garlic slices on medium heat.
4. Once the garlic is softened but not burnt, add the gochujang paste.
5. Lower the heat and let the gochujang infuse and release its flavours into the oil.
6. Add the double cream and mix well to combine the sauce. Turn the heat back up to medium and simmer the sauce until it reduces by half.
7. When the pasta is cooked, drain it but reserve half a cup of the water. Add the pasta and this water to the sauce and mix well.
8. Add the prawns and stir on the heat until they are almost cooked, then turn the heat to low.
9. Finally, add the butter and grated Parmesan and mix everything well to create a thick creamy sauce.
10. Taste and add more seasoning if necessary.
11. Transfer to a serving plate and sprinkle over a little more cheese and the chives or parsley.

Cooking time:
30 minutes

Spiciness:
medium to high

GOCHUJANG CHEESE AND COURGETTE STUFFED CHICKEN

This is a recipe I developed a few years back, and it has featured regularly on our table at home ever since. You can prepare a few of these chicken breasts in advance and keep in the fridge for a few days after marinating in gochujang sauce.

SERVES 2

- 2 chicken breasts
- Salt and pepper to season
- 100 g (3½ oz) grated mozzarella cheese
- ½ courgette (zucchini), sliced in rounds
- 8–10 basil leaves
- ½ can chopped tomatoes
- ½ tsp Asian chicken stock powder

Gochujang sauce

- 1 tbsp gochujang
- 1 tbsp soy sauce
- ½ tbsp garlic, crushed
- 2 tbsp tomato puree
- ½ tbsp brown sugar
- 1 tbsp paprika

METHOD

1. Preheat the oven to 180°C (350°F).
2. Take your chicken breasts and make a sideways slit in each one so one half can be opened up.
3. Season the chicken with salt and pepper and set aside for 10 minutes while you make the sauce.
4. Make the gochugang sauce by adding all of the ingredients to a small mixing bowl, and stirring them together well.
5. Take a brush, and brush this sauce all over the chicken inside and out.
6. Place the chicken breasts in a small deep baking tray and stuff the slit in each one with about half the cheese (reserving a little), about 5 courgette (zucchini) slices and 4 or 5 basil leaves. Close them over tightly – you can use a toothpick to help you do this.
7. If you have more courgette slices left, sprinkle them around the pan.
8. Pour over the can of chopped tomato, add the chicken stock powder and mix.
9. Sprinkle the reserved cheese on top of the chicken breast, cover the baking tray with foil and cook in the oven for 25–30 minutes. If you are using an air fryer, cook for 20 minutes.
10. Serve with an Italian salad and enjoy!

Cooking time: 15 minutes

Spiciness: medium

HAM AND CHEESE TOASTIES WITH KIMCHI

In the last few years, I have seen kimchi grilled cheese sandwiches in so many different places all over the UK. My local cheese shop sells them, and little food stalls at local markets have started making them too. If you still have not tried one yourself, I would strongly recommend that you do, especially when it involves nothing more than adding kimchi to your usual cheese toasties. I highly recommend using sourdough bread, however, as it is robust enough to take two strong-tasting ingredients: kimchi and cheese. There really is no excuse for not trying this latest trend. When you take your first bite, you will immediately understand why they are so popular. It just works.

MAKES 1 SANDWICH

Butter for spreading
2 slices of your favourite sourdough bread
100–120 g (3½–4½ oz) your favourite hard cheese or mix of cheeses
1 spring onion (scallion), stalk only, chopped
1 slice ham, torn into small pieces
80 g (3 oz) kimchi

TIP

With this toasted sandwich, the smellier and stronger the cheese, the better it is. Kimchi and strong cheese really complement each other's flavours.

METHOD

1. Butter the 'outside' of the bread.
2. Heat up a frying pan on a medium heat.
3. Place one slice of bread in the pan with the buttered side down.
4. Arrange the ingredients on the bread in the pan in this order: cheese, spring onion (scallion), ham, kimchi, cheese. Please ensure you have squeezed any juice from the kimchi – you don't want wet toasties!
5. Place the other slice of bread on top with the buttered side on the outside.
6. When the bread on the bottom gets nice and brown and the cheese starts melting, flip it over carefully.
7. Put a lid on the pan and continue on the heat for a minute or two, to encourage all of the cheese to melt.
8. When it's ready, slice it in half and serve with your favourite gherkin.

Cooking time:
20 minutes

Spiciness:
Mild

KIMCHI, CHEESE AND PRAWN FRITTERS WITH SWEETCORN

This is our third jeon/Korean fritter dish in this book, this time with a fusion twist. Whether you call them jeon or fritters, these culinary cousins are all delicious savoury comfort bites, perfect as snacks, starters or side dishes. The kimchi, prawn and cheese combination works wonderfully here, and the sweetcorn adds a refreshing crunch.

MAKES 6–7 FRITTERS

- 100 g (3½ oz) kimchi, juice squeezed out and chopped into small pieces
- 100 g (3½ oz) fresh or frozen prawns (shrimp), defrosted if needed and cut into 1-cm (9¾-in) pieces
- ⅓ onion (about 80 g/3 oz), finely chopped (can be replaced with extra kimchi)
- 60 g (2 oz) grated Cheddar cheese
- 80 g (3 oz) fresh or frozen sweetcorn
- 2 spring onions (scallions), stalks only, roughly chopped
- 100 g (3½ oz) plain (all-purpose) flour
- 2 medium (US large) eggs
- ½ tsp salt
- ⅓ tsp black pepper
- ½ tsp Dasida stock powder
- 3–4 tbsp vegetable oil

METHOD

1. Add the kimchi, prawns, onion, cheese, sweetcorn and spring onions to a mixing bowl.
2. Add the flour and eggs and season with salt, pepper and Dasida/chicken stock. Mix well.
3. Heat the vegetable oil in a frying pan on a medium heat.
4. Place a spoonful of the mix into the oil and shape into 10-cm (4-in) diameter pancakes. Cook on both sides until golden brown.
5. Enjoy these with the classic Korean dipping sauce (page 62), or experiment with your own favourite dipping sauce.

Cooking time: 30 minutes

Spiciness: mild

BREAKFAST ROLL KIMBAP

This is my take on the breakfast roll in kimbap style. The savoury taste of the sausage, eggs and cheese goes beautifully with salty and sweet carrots. You can get as creative as you like with kimbap, and adding some sautéed mushroom, spinach or bacon would work well too.

MAKES 2 ROLLS

- 400 g (14 oz) Korean steamed rice
- ⅓ tsp salt
- 2 tbsp sesame oil
- 1 tbsp roasted sesame seeds
- 3 medium (US large) eggs
- ½ large salad cucumber
- 1 large carrot (about 150 g/5½ oz), julienned
- 3 or 4 frankfurters
- 2 sheets seaweed for kimbap/sushi
- Salt and Korean black pepper for seasoning

METHOD

Prepare all the fillings as follows, season each with a pinch of salt and line them up on a large plate ready to be assembled.

1. **Rice:** Mix the hot steamed rice with salt, sesame oil and sesame seeds and set aside to cool down. Using it when too hot shrinks the seaweed and makes it soggy, making it impossible to roll properly.
2. **Egg sheet**: Beat the eggs with a pinch of salt. Heat a large frying pan on a low-medium heat with a spoonful of oil. Pour the beaten egg and let it cook slowly. When one side is almost cooked, you can turn off the heat and let the residue heat cook the egg sheet through. Move it to a chopping board and let it cool down before slicing it thinly.
3. **Cucumber:** If you are using English salad cucumber, scrape off the watery seedy part in the middle after slicing the cucumber in half lengthwise. Slice the cucumber halves lengthwise in fine strips. The length of the cucumber should be slightly longer than the rolls themselves.
4. **Carrot:** Lightly sauté the julienned carrot with a little oil in a frying pan. Season with 2–3 pinches of salt and black pepper. Cook only for a few minutes so it still has a crunch.
5. **Frankfurters:** If you manage to find thin ones about 1–1.5-cm (½-in) diameter, you can use them whole. If they are thicker than that, slice them in half. Just boil them for a few minutes and they are ready to be used.

ROLLING THE KIMBAP

1. Lay down your first of the 2 sheets of seaweed on a large chopping board, with the rough side facing up.
2. Spread out the rice as thinly as possible, leaving a 3-cm (1¼-in) gap at the top of the seaweed. This empty gap will act as a seal for the roll. Try to spread out the rice in an even thickness – this is a key to perfect looking kimbap.
3. Arrange half of all the fillings on the rice, positioning them slightly closer to your body, leaving yourself enough space to roll. For this kimbap, you will need one line of sausage, 3 strips of egg sheets, some cucumber strips and all of the carrots shared between the 2 rolls.
4. Once everything is lined up, grab the end of the seaweed closest to you and lift it up and over, covering the filling, holding all the fillings in place with your other fingers.
5. Once you are midway, switch your hand position and use your 4 fingers to roll and tuck in. When you do this, you are trying to compress all the fillings, keeping them all inside and rolled tight. A loose kimbap roll will crumble in pieces when sliced.
6. When you reach the end where you left a gap on the seaweed, hold the roll in place with one hand and dab a few drops of water with a brush on the seaweed, like applying glue.
7. When the water has soaked in a bit, finish rolling and leave it to rest with the connecting part facing down. The weight of the roll will keep the seaweed together until it sticks securely.
8. Brush a layer of sesame oil on the top half of the roll and slice using a bread knife. If you have a blunt knife you will end up squashing the roll and ruin the hard work.
9. Repeat with the second sheet of seaweed and the other half of the fillings.
10. Place the sliced kimbap on a plate and serve with a sprinkle of sesame seeds.

TIP

For obvious reasons, bacon and English sausages will work well as the filling for this breakfast roll kimbap!

Cooking time:
20 minutes

Spiciness:
mild

ROLLED EGGS WITH HAM AND SEAWEED

Rolled eggs are one of the most frequently featured items on Korean breakfast menus. To make a simple egg roll more nutritious, we add various fillings to the egg mix. I find the ham and eggs go together seamlessly, and the seaweed adds to this dish's savoury depth. It is tricky to roll these omelettes at first, but, like everything in life, keep practising and you will find your own little tricks to get it the way you want.

SERVES 2–3 PEOPLE

5 medium (US large) eggs
40 g (1½ oz) ham, diced
½ tsp salt
½ tsp Korean black pepper
a few shakes Ajinomoto
2 sheets seaweed, cut in half
Neutral vegetable oil for frying

METHOD

1. Beat the eggs in a measuring jug.
2. Add the ham, salt, pepper and Ajinomoto and mix well.
3. In a medium-sized frying pan or egg roll pan, add some oil and heat on medium.
4. Pour in about 2–3 tbsp of egg mix and let it spread out to fill the pan.
5. When almost cooked through, start rolling up the egg pancake from one end of the pan and keep rolling until you have reached the other side.
6. Slide the egg to the side you started to roll from, add some more oil and pour in another 2–3 tbsp of egg mix.
7. Spread the egg mix thinly and this time place a sheet of seaweed over the top.
8. Start rolling, and when the sheet of seaweed is completely rolled into the omelette, place another sheet and keep rolling.
9. With the seaweed, you will see a bright black line going around the egg roll.
10. Repeat this process with 2 or 3 sheets of seaweed until you use up all the egg mix.
11. Move the roll to a chopping board and let it cool down before you start slicing it.
12. Serve with some salad as a wholesome breakfast or lunch.

Cooking time:
1 hour

Spiciness:
medium

KOREAN BBQ PULLED PORK SANDWICH WITH QUICK KIMCHI

The grand finale of the Korean fusion dishes is the king of sandwiches: a pulled pork sandwich with a Korean twist. I thought of this dish straight away when I decided to dedicate a chapter to Korean Fusion food and wanted to save it to last and end the book with a bang!

I almost think this version of the sandwich is better than the original. Korean pulled pork is less sweet than other versions so the meat can be better appreciated, and the marriage with the quick pickled cucumber and carrot kimchi salad is perfect.

MAKES 4–5 SANDWICHES

Pork filling

500 g (1 lb 2 oz) pork shoulder
300 ml (10 fl oz) chicken stock
2 tbsp gochujang
2 tbsp honey
1 tbsp sugar
2 tbsp soy sauce
½ tsp five spice
½ tbsp garlic, crushed
1 tsp ginger, grated
Salt and pepper to your taste.
2–3 spring onions (scallions), stalks only, roughly chopped

Quick pickled cucumber and carrot

½ cucumber (about 150 g/5½ oz), julienned
1 small carrot (about 100 g/3½ oz), julienned
2 tbsp rice vinegar
1 tbsp sugar
2–3 pinches salt
1 tsp fine gochugaru
1 tbsp fish sauce
1 tsp garlic, minced

Kimchi mayo

2 tbsp kimchi juice
2 tbsp mayonnaise

Sandwich

4 brioche buns, buttered
Handful mint leaves

METHOD

1. Preheat the oven to 135°C (275°F).
2. Prepare the meat by seasoning with salt and pepper and placing in a heavy-based lidded casserole.
3. Add all remaining ingredients for the pork except the spring onions (scallions) and mix well. Close the lid.
4. Cook in the oven for 4–5 hours or, if you have a slow cooker, use it on a pulled pork setting.
5. When the meat is ready, mix in the chopped spring onions and shred it with two forks.
6. Meanwhile, prep the carrot and cucumber and mix well with all of the

other pickle ingredients.

7. Set aside, ready to be used when putting together the sandwich, squeezing out some of the water just before doing so.
8. Mix the Kimchi juice and mayonnaise together to make the kimchi mayo.
9. To assemble the sandwich, butter the brioche and grill lightly on a dry pan to colour.
10. Spread on some kimchi mayo and 2–3 tbsp of the pulled pork. Add some of the pickled cucumber and carrot, close the bun and enjoy!

INDEX

D

E

F

G

H

R

S

T

V

Y

AUTHOR'S NOTE

I am thrilled to be part of your Korean cooking adventure, whether this is your first introduction to Korean food or you're a lifelong fan.

I have always been a food lover, but it was when I became a mother that my passion for cooking, rather than just eating, was ignited. Having moved to the UK in my mid-teens, the diverse food scene here was like a playground for me, and it allowed me to reimagine Korean food in new and exciting ways. I hope this is a cookbook that will take you on a similar, horizon-expanding journey, and by the end of it you will have a better understanding of what Korean food is all about and how to enjoy it fully.

This book is the culmination of years of cooking, experimenting and – thankfully! – eating, and creating it has been a total delight. I sincerely hope you can feel that fun in every recipe. Share these dishes with your loved ones and create your own delicious, lasting memories.

With love,

Haebin x